KU-289-593

JEWISH
MANCHESTER
AN ILLUSTRATED HISTORY
BILL WILLIAMS

JEWISH
MANCHESTER
AN ILLUSTRATED HISTORY
BILL WILLIAMS

breedon **books**
PUBLISHING

First published in Great Britain in 2008 by
The Breedon Books Publishing Company Limited
Breedon House, 3 The Parker Centre,
Derby, DE21 4SZ.

© BILL WILLIAMS, 2008

All Rights Reserved. No part of this publication may be
reproduced, stored in a retrieval system, or transmitted in any
form, or by any means, electronic, mechanical, photocopying,
recording or otherwise without the prior permission in writing
of the copyright holders, nor be otherwise circulated in any
form or binding or cover other than in which it is published
and without a similar condition being imposed on the
subsequent publisher.

ISBN: 978-1-85983-615-6

Printed and bound by Cromwell Press Ltd.
Trowbridge, Wiltshire.

Contents

Introduction

Manchester Jewry is today the largest Jewish community in the British provinces, with a population conservatively estimated at 35,000. It is served by around 46 synagogues, which between them represent every religious segment of British Jewry, and by over 150 other institutions that provide for the community's cultural, social, educational, political and charitable needs. This includes 20 Zionist organisations, which highlight Manchester Jewry's support of the State of Israel. It has its own newspaper, The Jewish Telegraph, founded in 1950, which serves as a major vehicle of communication within the community. It was Manchester's largest minority community until the arrival of immigrants from the British Commonwealth in the years after World War Two. It was also a community of international importance, consisting of immigrants and refugees from almost every part of the Jewish world, reflecting all the major developments in Jewish communities overseas and itself playing a major role in the evolution of world Jewry. It was in Manchester that Chaim Weitzmann, a lecturer in Chemistry at the University of Manchester, created the band of Zionists, the so-called 'Manchester School', that subsequently played a major role in persuading the British Government to issue the Balfour Declaration, on which the creation of the State of Israel was to be substantially based.

Locally, as merchants, industrialists and shopkeepers; doctors, dentists, lawyers and academics; musicians, artists and architects; city councillors and civic administrators; and as the founders, patrons and managers of local charities, members of the community have played major roles in the economic, cultural and political development of Manchester and Salford since the late 18th century. The community and the city have grown in parallel, chiefly in harmony, with each feeding off the other to generate both new ideas and fresh initiatives. Jewish Mancunians have prided themselves and have, in turn, been appreciated as striking a careful balance between their membership of a community, with its own distinct ideals, and their commitment to the affairs of the city and the nation. Sir Sidney Hamburger, born in Manchester of immigrant parents, combined his accepted leadership of the Jewish community with the Mayoralty of Salford and the chairmanship of the North Western Health Authority (1973–82), for which he was honoured with a knighthood. The City of Manchester's current chief executive, Sir Howard Bernstein, while active in Jewish communal affairs, was knighted in 2003 for 'services to Manchester', which included the planning of the 2002 Commonwealth Games in the city. He remains a central figure in the progressive regeneration of Manchester.

The word 'community' perhaps requires some explanation. The 'Jewish community' is a voluntary society of those who believe themselves to have something in common as Jews. Membership of the 'community' chiefly expresses itself in terms of allegiance to institutions based on such presumed commonality. At first, in 18th and early 19th century Manchester, this was a shared commitment to Judaism and its expression typically took the form of membership of a synagogue, which allowed participation in Jewish rituals and through which the right to a Jewish marriage and burial might also be attained. As time went on, however, there evolved other ways of being 'Jewish', and of expressing 'Jewishness', which had little or nothing to do with religion. There were those who, while abandoning religious belief, maintained a sense of a shared historical heritage and who might occasionally observe Jewish festivals, by a more or less perfunctory attendance at synagogue, or maintain one or other of the Jewish domestic rituals such as the Sabbath meal or a Seder at Passover. Others, including some who converted to Christianity, indulged what can only be described as a nostalgia for their Jewish roots by occasionally contributing to Jewish causes, for example, donating to one of Manchester's Jewish charities or speaking out against anti-Semitic abuse. Jewishness might also arise from a sense of shared victimhood; Jewish working men, some of them committed to atheistic socialism, created trade unions in the early 1890s, which were Jewish either in name or in the character of their memberships and which sought to limit their exploitation, sometimes by Jewish bosses. Once Zionism had taken root in the late 19th century, there were those whose Jewishness took the form of a shared nationality, expressing itself in membership of one of Manchester's many Zionist organisations or, in 1967 for example, lending support to the Jewish state. A Manchester 'Jewish ethnic identity' might be made up of a variety of mixtures of some or all of these elements.

The subjects of this book are those who saw themselves as part of an 'organised' community and who thus participated, as givers or receivers, in Jewish organisations, religious, political, social or cultural. Throughout the 200 years which this book covers, however, there were always people of Jewish origin who, for reasons of conversion, out-marriage, apathy or personal non-conformity, cut off all their links with an organised 'community'. Such people, even if Jewish in accordance with Jewish religious law, have typically been omitted from any 'count' or estimate of the 'Jewish' population. Jewish population figures, even when based on a careful analysis of census returns, are thus always an underestimate of those of Jewish origin living in the city and of 'Jewish' contributions to civic life.

Although held together organisationally after 1919 by a Jewish Representative Council, and throwing up communal 'leaders', some self-proclaimed, some based on their acceptance by this or that section of the community, some with a brief which came to extend over the community as a whole, the community was never either homogenous or united. It was divided, like any other society, in terms of the national origins, religious preferences, political allegiances, economic achievements and social class of its members. There were also personal differences, some creating fierce clashes in what was, as in any other society, a constant search by the ambitious for prestige and power. The term 'macher', literally 'maker', has been coined to describe (sometimes disparagingly) the more aspiring communal activist, anxious to leave his (or her) mark on the community. All these differences played a central role in communal history. They help explain, among other things, the diversity of synagogues, the divergent patterns of settlement, and the tensions and conflicts which puncture communal history. It might be argued that it is these differences, and their expression, which give vitality to communal history and which often underpin the community's religious evolution. The 'community' was (and is) a complex living organism in the process of constant change to which no linear narrative can do adequate justice.

It is my hope that the brief history that follows embraces both the major signposts of change in Manchester's Jewish history and the diverse historical ingredients which make up the Jewish community of today, and that it adequately reflects my own admiration for the struggles and achievements of the Jewish people.

Note:
The meaning of words *italicised* at their first use in the text will be found in the glossary at the back of the book.

Acknowledgements

Members of the Manchester Jewish community have, with considerable generosity, long extended to me, an outsider, a welcome as an historian interested in their local history. Without such a welcome, it would have been imposssible for me to attempt to understand and evaluate their rich and many-sided heritage. For this I am truly grateful. The study of local Jewish history has given meaning to my life over the last 30 years and I trust that it has proved helpful to the community.

I am grateful to the holders of the copyright to the photgraphs included in this book – the Manchester Jewish Museum, the Local Studies Department of Manchester Central Library, Jewish Heritage UK, Mr Michael Poloway and Mr Merton Paul – for permission to reproduce them. The photographs taken by Mr Poloway have recently formed the basis of a highly successul exhibition at the Manchester Jewish Museum, while Mr Paul has taken the initiative in recording the redevopment of the former areas of Jewish residence.

I am also grateful to Dr Sharman Kadish, Director of the Survey of the Jewish Built Heritage in the UK and Ireland, set up in 1997, with the support of English Heritage and the Heritage Lottery Fund, to record the architectural history of British Jewry. It was through Dr Kadish that I have gained access to a series of photographs of Manchester Jewish buildings acquired by the Manchester residents, Tony and Dawn Glyn, from an auction in Chicago. Taken in the first decade of the 20th century, these photographs, published here for the first time, illustrate important buildings subsequently demolished and hitherto without illustrated trace. They are credited to the Glyn family and to Jewish Heritage UK, of which Dr Kadish is also the director.

Finally, my thanks go out to my good Manchester friends, David Arnold and Merton and Barbara Paul for reading an early draft of this book and for their helpful comments.

The errors are all mine.

Bill Williams
February 2008.

Chapter 1

The Origins of the Community, 1740–1858

Pedlars, Shopkeepers and Merchants

Although Jewish traders had settled in British towns like London, Norwich, Lincoln and York during the Middle Ages, Manchester at that time was of too little economic importance to attract them. Manchester's Jewish community took shape only in the 1780s as the town began to evolve as a major centre for the production and trade in cotton textiles. Like many other Jewish communities in Britain, it was the creation of itinerant traders who during the first half of the 18th century began to reach out from their bases in London and the south coast in search of new markets in the British provinces. Most were of German origin and of fairly recent arrival in Britain, where they had hoped to extend their commercial opportunities. The goods that they carried in packs or trays were those which were readily portable, which might be replenished in the course of their journeys and which were in popular demand: such items as jewellery, pens and pencils, ostrich feathers, straw hats, brushes, umbrellas, optical lenses, patent medicines and second-hand clothing. There were also

18th-century woodcut showing a Jewish old clothes dealer purchasing from a servant the cast-off garments of his master.

Jewish travellers who offered rudimentary services as pawnbrokers, opticians, dentists and (typically quack) doctors, particularly to those out of reach of Britain's urban centres. Before setting out on their journeys, those who were religiously observant would agree to meet on the Jewish Sabbath at prearranged lodging houses, warehouses or shops to form the necessary *minyan* of 10 adult males for public worship, before moving on to their next port of call when the Sabbath ended. Lodging-house keepers accustomed to accommodating them are said to have kept a special cupboard for cooking utensils which enabled the pedlars to prepare *kosher* food. Such travelling *minyanim* might include a man skilled as a *Reader* to lead the service and another trained as a *shochet* to provide kosher meat.

The earliest evidence of Jewish contacts with Manchester suggests that one such 'brotherhood' had begun to trade in the town by 1740, just as it had begun to emerge as 'a spacious, rich and populous' centre for the manufacture of linen and cotton goods. A town plan of that time is surrounded by pictures of the 'elegant and magnificent mansions' of merchants and manufacturers who dominated a town of perhaps 15,000 people and of St Ann's Church, then in the process of construction. On 26 February 1740, a notice was placed in the *London Gazette* by a Jewish hawker of jewellery, one Isaac Solomon, who claimed to have been robbed by highwaymen on the road between Manchester and Rochdale, and who described his assailants in the hope of their apprehension and the goods which had been stolen in the hope of their recovery. Apart from gold and silver coins, he had lost silver rings, shoe buckles, tea tongs, watch chains and snuff boxes valued, according to his advertisement, at '£10 and upwards': the kinds of goods, that is, likely to have been within the means of Manchester's small but prospering middle classes. Who he was, where he came from and what happened to him are not known, but his presence some six or seven miles out of Manchester suggests that the town had, by 1740, become a target for a higher echelon of Jewish travellers. The presence on a town plan published in 1741 of a small alleyway known as 'Synagogue Alley', running off Deansgate in central Manchester, may suggest the site not of a synagogue, but of a shop or warehouse where a group of Jewish travellers, passing through Manchester and staying at local inns, held their Sabbath services.

There is evidence that, within the three decades which followed, the number of Jewish pedlars visiting the city had begun to increase. In 1774 a notice appeared in local newspaper accusing 'Jews and other foreigners' of coming to the town as industrial spies, intent on selling the new secrets of the cotton industry to Britain's overseas competitors, and offering a reward to anyone who identified a foreigner so engaged. While there is no proof of Jewish industrial espionage, the notice suggests that Jewish pedlars were then sufficiently familiar in the locality to lend a degree of credence to such an accusation. The chances are, however, that like the Italian pedlars visiting Manchester at the same time, and selling optical instruments, picture frames, prints and plaster figurines, they were attracted to a town in which the consumer market was growing annually. By the late 1770s, contact with Manchester had also been made by a group of Jewish pedlars, some of whom had settled 20 years earlier in Liverpool.

It was this 'Liverpool connection' which appears to have spearheaded Jewish settlement in Manchester in the late 1780s, when the town's population had risen to over 42,000 in the wake of the expansion of the cotton industry. The leaders of these first Jewish colonists were the brothers Lemon and Jacob Nathan, immigrants to Britain from Bavaria, who had settled in Liverpool as dealers in second-hand clothes (known at the time as 'slop-sellers') and who had moved on to Manchester in or about 1788. They brought with them some 10 to 15 other families, most of them from Liverpool, all of them having only recently exchanged the itinerant trades for settled shopkeeping. They included

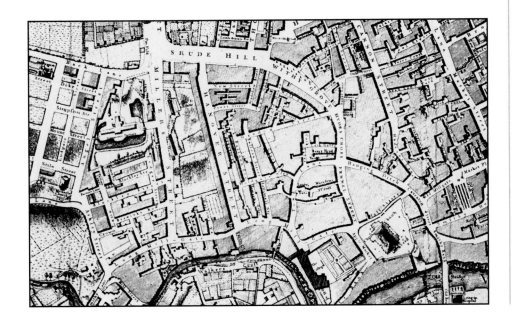

The 'Old Town,' the site of Manchester's first area of Jewish residence, from a town plan of 1790.

Postcard of 'Poet's Corner' in Long Millgate, c.1890, marked with a cross by Elias Nathan to indicate the premises which had been the shop of his father and uncle, Jacob and Lemon Nathan, at No. 144.

a salesman of patent medicines, dealers in ostrich feathers, straw hats, stationery, jewellery, watches, umbrellas and optical lenses, slop-sellers, and a 'travelling corn-curer' who was also a dentist. Another was the umbrella dealer Mordecai Slazenger Moss, whose descendants were to create the Slazenger tennis racket. Although others may have made an individual choice to join them, they appear to have arrived as a group and to have very rapidly set about building the rudiments of a Jewish community. In 1794 the Nathan brothers began paying for the lease of a small plot of land attached to a Christian cemetery in Whit Lane, Pendleton, for use as a burial ground. Two years later they were paying rent for a room in a warehouse in Garden Street, off Withy Grove, for use as a place of worship. At this Garden Street 'synagogue', one of the pioneers, Aaron Jacob, a slop-seller by trade, served as Reader and shochet.

Members of the 'colony' had opened shops in and around an area of central Manchester known as the 'Old Town', a district of black and white timbered housing dating from the Elizabethan era, encompassed by Shude Hill, Withy Grove and what was then Miller's Lane (now Miller Street). In the 1780s it was in a state of decay as factories, warehouses and jerry-built slum property had begun to surround it on all sides. It was for this reason that the new settlers were able to acquire relatively large

Advert for the shop of Elias Nathan, son of Jacob Nathan.

property at relatively low rent. It was also a maze of alleys and courts in which Jewish settlers, understandably fearful of anti-Jewish feeling, might trade with working-class customers without attracting too much public attention. The Nathan brothers opened their shop at 144 Long Millgate, a timbered building opposite the gates of Chetham's College, where they gradually increased the scope of their enterprise to jewellery, watches and pawn-broking. Until the late 1790s Manchester Jewry comprised perhaps 15 families engaged in petty commerce in the back streets of central Manchester, worshipping together in the back room of a warehouse and burying their dead in Pendleton, some four miles away in Salford, the only land they had been able to rent at a time of wide-spread suspicion of Jews. One of the few surviving memorial stones, dating from 1798, records the death of Henry, the infant son of Dr Samuel Solomon, a notorious and highly successful quack doctor of Liverpool whose brother had settled in Manchester, and who may have found, in the new Jewish shops, an avenue for the distribution of his patent medicines, which included 'Solomon Drops' and the then famous 'Balm of Gilead.'

A PILLAR of the EXCHANGE

Nathan Rothschild at his favoured pillar in the London Exchange after leaving Manchester in 1810.

Barred by ancient prejudice from most other centres of local society in Liverpool and Manchester, some of the earliest Jewish settlers, including the Nathan brothers, had joined Freemason lodges, open without religious restriction, as a means of relating to the local populations and perhaps of confirming their own commercial integrity. Certificates survive showing that Lemon Nathan had belonged to a Freemason lodge in Liverpool before coming to Manchester and that Jacob Franks, a dealer in optical lenses, who had arrived in Manchester with the Nathan brothers and was one of the signatories of the

Trade card of Nathan Mayer Rothschild during his time in Manchester as a cotton merchant. Although describing himself as a 'manufacturer,' he obtained his goods from cotton mills in and around Manchester for export to his father in Frankfurt.

lease of the Pendleton Burial Ground, joined a Manchester lodge in 1810. Aaron Jacob, Reader at the first Manchester synagogue, was also a Freemason. Jacob Nathan's son Elias, who became an optician, was also a manufacturer of Masonic jewellery. The other focus of the colony's social life, apart from the synagogue, was the kosher restaurant opened on Long Millgate in 1819 by Sarah Levy.

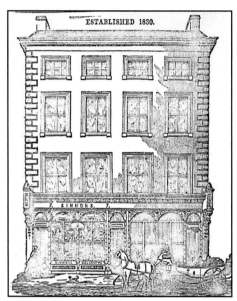

The jewellery shop of Isaac Simmons in St Ann's Square, 1835.

Advertisement for Isaac Simmons's shop, c.1835, suggesting that, like other Jewish shopkeepers, he was now dealing with a middle-class clientele.

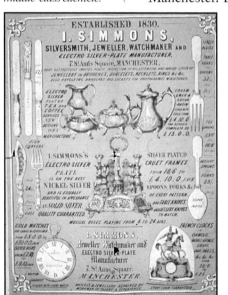

In 1799 these ex-pedlars making their way into the Manchester economy with mixed fortunes were joined by a Jewish immigrant from Frankfurt, whose ambitions stretched well beyond the retail trades. Nathan Mayer Rothschild, who then established himself in Manchester as a cotton merchant, was the son of Amschel Rothschild of Frankfurt who, to extend his already extensive commercial interests, had despatched his sons to centres of trade throughout Europe. In Manchester, where he acquired a house at Downing Street, Ardwick, some two miles from the Old Town, and a warehouse in Mosley Street in the town centre, Nathan Rothschild bought in cotton cloth from factories around Manchester for export to his home country. A surviving day book records his purchases and profits and notes the cases of wine with which he encouraged his suppliers. It is said that, in his 10 years in Manchester, he tripled his initial investment of around £20,000 before moving to London, where in 1810 he established the family's merchant bank in New Court.

The export of cotton goods and the retailing of what became the Jewish staple products – clothing, jewellery and stationery – were the economic bases around which the Jewish community evolved. The early success of some of the Old Town shops encouraged other pedlars to settle with their co-religionists in Manchester. By the 1830s, the more successful of those pioneer shopkeepers, doctors and opticians had themselves begun to move from the back streets to the improved shopping districts around Deansgate, Market Street and St Ann's Square, upgrading their goods and services, and exchanging working-class for middle-class customers. In 1832 Isaac Simmons, son of the travelling 'dentist and corn extractor', opened a jewellery shop which still stands in St Ann's Square. At the same time, the success of Nathan Rothschild in the cotton trade had begun to attract *Ashkenazi* traders from Germany and Holland, and *Sephardi* merchants from the Mediterranean coastlands to Manchester, itself now fast becoming the centre of the world's textile trade. One of the first of the Ashkenazi traders was Solomon Levi Behrens of Hamburg, who had business connections with the

Rothschilds in Frankfurt and who moved to Manchester as a manufacturer and exporter of cotton textiles in 1814. The first Sephardi merchants arrived in Manchester in the 1840s at first as the visiting agents of family firms, based in Gibraltar, Constantinople, Morocco and Syria, and then, increasingly from the 1860s, as permanent settlers with warehouses in central Manchester.

Shop of Benjamin Hyam in Market Street, 1851. The first shop in Manchester (and possibly in Britain) to sell ready-made clothes.

Pioneer Jewish shopkeepers and merchants were operating in what was becoming the world's first industrial city: the 'shock city of the age', in which what we now know as 'modern urban life' was taking shape for the first time. Visitors came to Manchester from far and wide to view the novelties of urban living, working and leisure. Manchester's Market Street was described by one of them in 1830 as 'the most handsome shopping street in Europe'. Its palatial shops included one set up by Benjamin Hyam, a former Jewish hawker of old clothes, who in 1832 arrived in Manchester from Ipswich to establish his 'Pantechnethica', probably the world's first shop to make and sell ready-made suits. It seems that Hyam would deliver cloth to poorer Manchester families who were expected to make it up to his specifications. So novel was his trade that when the Manchester Poor Law authorities sought to attract workers from rural districts to the cotton

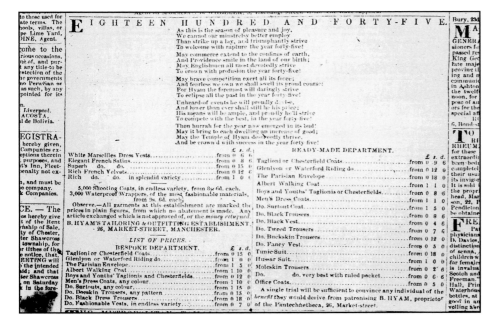

Typical advertising poem by Benjamin Hyam, in the Manchester Guardian of January 1845.

warehouses in 1832, their propaganda included the prices of Hyam's suits. Hyam himself advertised his enterprise – the 'Temple of Hyam' – in verse which sometimes occupied a complete column of the *Manchester Guardian*. Whenever prestigious visitors came to Manchester, Charles Dickens, for example, or the Italian nationalist, Mazzini, Hyam's verse would record their (invariably good) impressions of his Market Street 'Temple'. His movement from second-hand clothing to bespoke and ready-made wear was followed by all except the very poorest of his Jewish contemporary slop-sellers in

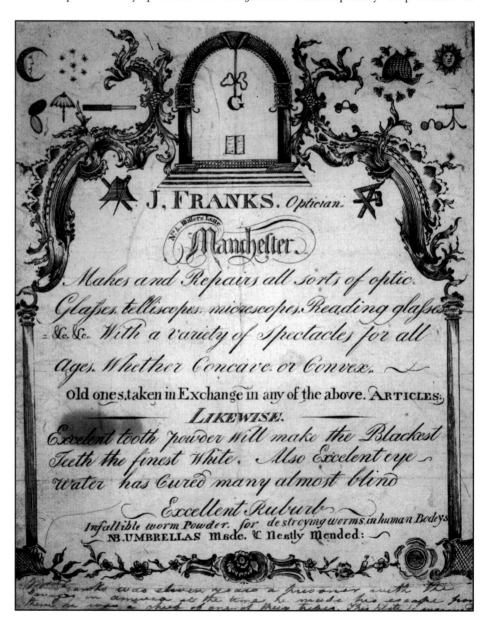

Trade card of Jacob Franks, one of the founders of Manchester Jewry, c.1810. Jacob Franks married twice and had 24 children. All his sons became opticians.

Manchester, the monopoly of dealing in second-hand clothing passing to the Irish.

Hyam's was only one of many of the contributions which Jewish entrepreneurs were making to the economic growth of the town. The jewellery and stationery trades were equally reshaped for a middle-class clientele by Jewish enterprise. From the 1830s, Jewish export merchants in Manchester, now housed in their own premises in Manchester's warehouse district, were playing an increasingly important role in extending the markets for Manchester goods in Europe, Asia and South America. Between 1836 and 1843, of 28 Jewish cotton merchants settled in Manchester, 26 were from Germany and Holland and two from the Mediterranean world: Samuel Hadida from Gibraltar and Abraham Nissim Levy from Constantinople. Jewish opticians descended from the 18th century's dealers in optical lenses and were helping to create what was becoming a

FRANKS'S
BRAZILIAN PEBBLE
SPECTACLES,
With the decidedly great advantage of proper adaptation
TO PRESERVE SIGHT,
Or to Remedy the Inconvenience of Defective Vision,
MAY BE OBTAINED AT THE
OPTICAL MANUFACTURING ESTABLISHMENTS,
114, DEANSGATE,
Next Door to the Star Hotel, near the corner of King Street, and
44, Market Street, Manchester.

CAUTION.—The celebrity of the above establishments has induced persons, well dressed or otherwise, to practise calling at the houses in Manchester and the neighbouring towns, with circulars or handbills, and, subsequently, with spectacles for sale, who represent themselves as in some way connected with the Messrs. FRANKS, or as having worked for them, and even to the impertinent extent of being related to them. Messrs. FRANKS, therefore, respectfully intimate that they do not themselves travel, neither do they employ any person to do so, nor do they supply goods for that purpose.

BRAZILIAN PEBBLE SPECTACLES,
IN BLUE STEEL FRAMES,
Such as are usually sold at 10s. 6d. will be supplied at 6s. 6d.; and such as are usually sold at 21s. will be adapted at 14s. 6d. by
A. AND J. FRANKS,
CONSULTING AND MANUFACTURING OPTICIANS,
Lecturers on the "Anatomy and Physiology of the Human Eye," and of the "Use and Abuse of Spectacles."
Authors of "Anatomical Delineations of the Eye-Ball, &c. &c.

Advertisement for the shop of Jacob Franks's sons, Abraham and Joseph. Note their distancing of themselves from the travelling opticians (including their father) of an earlier age. They portray themselves as skilled professional opticians.

scientific profession. An advertising sheet distributed in 1810, by Jacob Franks, suggests the high degree of his versatility and the rather lower level of his professional skill: 'J. Franks, Optician, Miller's Lane, Manchester. Makes and Repairs all sorts of optical glasses, telliscopes, microscopes. Reading glasses etc. etc. With a variety of spectacles for all ages, whether Concave or Convex. Old ones taken in exchange for any of the above articles. Likewise Excelent tooth powder will make the blackest teeth the finest white. Also excellent eye-water has cured many almost blind. Excellent rubarb. Infallible worm powders for destroying worms in human bodys. NB. Umbrellas made and neatly mended.'

Two of Jacob Franks's sons, however, acquired premises in Deansgate where they manufactured and sold spectacles and other optical instruments of high quality, some of them now in the Manchester Museum of Science and Industry. They gave public lectures on demand, wrote short but serious pamphlets on diseases of the eye and served as consultants to the new, and highly reputable, Manchester Eye Hospital.

Elias Nathan and his family in the 1890s, after their move to a cottage in Cheetwood, Cheetham Hill.

The Jewish Quarter

As their economic and professional status improved, Jewish settlers began to move out of an increasingly polluted and disease-ridden city centre towards the rural outskirts of Manchester, which were developing as the world's first urban 'suburbs', leaving their premises to be guarded overnight by watchmen. Most moved northwards into the salubrious and still largely rural Cheetham Hill and Broughton districts of the town. The tailor, Benjamin Hyam, built himself a cottage on the Cliff in Higher Broughton (when he left for London during the 1860s, he changed his surname to 'Halford', retaining, that is, the 'H' of Hyam and the 'alford' of Salford); the optician Abraham Franklin, who had also begun life as a pedlar of lenses, before settling in Manchester in 1823 and opening a shop in St Ann's Square, additionally built a house at the junction of Broughton Lane and Great Ducie Street, Strangeways, a desireable address in 1834. One of the most prominent Jewish textile manufacturers and exporters, Philip Lucas, acquired a palatial home, Temple House, in the upper reaches of Cheetham Hill, surrounded by woodland and lakes. Lesser traders rented villas on or near Cheetham Hill Road. Others, fewer in number, but from similar echelons of traders and professionals, moved to the south of the town, to villas in the area of All Saints, Longsight, Chorlton-on-Medlock and Victoria Park. Solomon Levi Behrens was alone in having accumulated sufficient wealth to purchase an estate of 50 acres at Catteral near Garstang where, while still retaining his Jewish religious observances, he lived out his life as a country gentleman.

The institutions of the community followed the ascent to wealth and status of its leading merchants and shopkeepers. The Nathan brothers' leadership gave way to an elite of overseas merchants and major shopkeepers to whom the first rudimentary institutions of the community were no longer acceptable. The community's place of worship, after moving in 1806 from Garden Street to a converted warehouse in Ainsworth's Court off Long Millgate, moved in 1824 to a neat, if unspectacular, custom-built synagogue in Halliwell Street, close to what is now Victoria Station, which cost the community £1,700 to build. Attached to it was a small school at which the children of the community learnt the rudiments of Hebrew and Judaism. In 1826 the community opened its first communal charity, the Manchester Hebrew Philanthropic Society, modelled closely on a similar institution in Liverpool, which provided weekly pensions to widows, orphans, the sick and the infirm, between Jewish New Year and Passover.

The Manchester Hebrew Association

Leading Jewish merchants and shopkeepers in Manchester also began to see themselves as an influential pressure group within British Jewry. In October 1838, 12 of them, including Benjamin Hyam and Philip Lucas, met at the house of the jeweller and optician, Abraham Franklin, on Broughton Lane, to found a Manchester Hebrew Association. Its stated aim was 'to promote a due appreciation of the Jewish religion and its morality [and] the spiritual and intellectual advancement of its members'. In a wider reality, its purpose was to add its weight to the movement for Jewish political emancipation which had recently begun in London, following the grant of political rights to Roman Catholics in 1829. The intent of the Association was to improve the standing of Manchester's Jewish institutions and the 'respectability' of the Jewish population so as to 'prove' the community 'ready' to take part in the government of a Christian country. This included the initiation of the first sermons in English at the Halliwell Street Synagogue and, more importantly, the education of the Jewish poor.

The progress of the Manchester Hebrew Association, under the presidency of Philip Lucas, is recorded in a scroll buried in a bottle in 1858, with copies of Jewish newspapers, under the foundation stone of the Great Synagogue and recovered only in the early 1980s after the synagogue's demolition. In 1838 Revd David Meyer Isaacs, the minister of a Liverpool synagogue, was appointed on a part-time basis to deliver 'lectures' in English at Halliwell Street. Finding that 'twenty-five [Jewish] children of both sexes aged 4–15' were 'as yet uneducated', the Association (later changing its name to the Hebrew Education Society) accorded

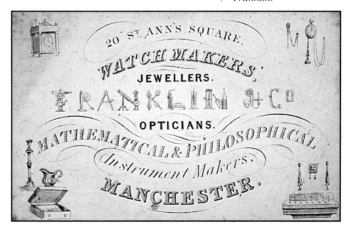

Trade card of Abraham Franklin.

priority to finding school places for as many of these children as possible. In 1840 it paid 4d a child for 12 children to attend the small private school of a Mr Corns in Redfern Street, off Miller Street. While Mr Corns provided 'the elements of an English education', a Jewish teacher was appointed part-time to provide an education in Hebrew. In November 1842, as the number of Jewish pupils increased, rooms were engaged at the Salford Lyceum for an independent Jewish school with a Mr Asher as its headmaster, a Mr Duffield as an English teacher and a Mrs Solomons as 'Governess' to teach sewing to the girls. After two years of experiment, in November 1846 a house was 'taken up' and furnished in Hanover Street where, for three years, an average of 70 children received an education in English and Hebrew.

This was such a success that, in March 1849, Philip Lucas launched an appeal for funds to create a purpose-built school. Within six months, according to the recovered scroll, £1,462 had been raised not only from local Jews but 'from men of all religious denominations in Manchester' and several Jewish donors from London, Birmingham and Liverpool. In October 1850, land belonging to the local Jewish jeweller Louis Beaver, on Cheetham Hill Road, was purchased and, on 22 May 1851, the first Manchester Jews' School was built on the site (78 Cheetham Hill Road) to the design of the prominent local architect John Edgar Gregan.

Those who had put up the money for the building of the Halliwell Street Synagogue, who had founded the Hebrew Philanthropic Society and the Hebrew Association, and who had created, and now managed, the Manchester Jews' School had, by 1840, begun to see themselves as part of the middle class of the 'New Athens'. They had their photographs taken by leading Manchester studios in the archetypal poses of the bourgeoisie and their pictures painted in oils by prominent local artists. Apart from Freemasons' lodges, they now belonged to Manchester's leading social clubs and cultural societies. One Jewish calico printer of German origin, Salis Schwabe, who had built an impressive calico printing works in Rhodes near Manchester, lived in a mansion in north Manchester called Crumpsall Hall, where he held soirées for the Manchester elite and a musical evening which included pieces by the young composer, Chopin, who was visiting Manchester. In a bust, created by a local sculptor, Schwabe is depicted wearing a (no doubt Athenian) toga. Members of the Behrens family joined the Cheshire Hunt and socialised at the home of the

novelist Elizabeth Gaskell, on Plymouth Grove, who employed a German-Jewish teacher of languages, Tobias Theodores, as a tutor for one of her children. During the 1840s Edward Salomon, the son of a Jewish cotton merchant, was at the beginning of his career as a prominent local architect. Abraham Franklin's son, Jacob, after receiving his education from the Manchester Mechanics Institute, left Manchester for London where, in 1841, he created the first Jewish national newspaper, *The Voice of Jacob*. His brother, Isaac Abraham Franklin, in 1835 became a surgeon in Manchester, where he served the town authorities in dealing with lethal outbreaks of cholera. Leading Jewish shopkeepers, like Jacob Franks's eldest sons, distanced themselves in their advertisements from rough 'travellers' dealing (as their own father had done) in similar products. Jacob Nathan sent two of his sons to Manchester Grammar School from where one, Lewis Henry Nathan, went to train as a surgeon at University College, London. It appears, too, that middle-class Jews were now accepted by middle-class Manchester. They were praised for their respectability, their sobriety, their respect for the law, their civic-mindedness, patriotism and 'Englishness' by their Manchester peers in the pages of the *Manchester Guardian* and from the platform of the Free Trade Hall. It seems likely that the social eminence and the conspicuous integration of its leading members spared the community's poor popular abuse, which was levelled instead at Manchester's growing number of Irish settlers.

Synagogal Rebellion

The local Jewish elite had also taken control of the Halliwell Street Synagogue as its 'Free (that is, privileged) Members'. Only they were allowed a vote at the synagogue's general meetings, which determined changes to the ritual of the congregation, appointed its salaried officials and elected the members of a governing 'Select Committee'. Members of the body of the congregation could become 'Free Members' only after five years residence in Manchester and then only with the approval of the 'Select Committee'. Even in the burial ground, which had moved in 1840 from Pendleton to a site in Prestwich, ordinary seatholders were separated from the plots reserved for 'Free Members'. By 1844 such a structure had become unacceptable to the many new shopkeepers arriving in the town, whose 'seat rents' gave them no right to a vote in synagogue affairs and many of whom had absorbed the democratic ideals of British society, which had culminated in the Reform Act. In that year they launched a democratic rebellion under the leadership of a newly arrived German shirt manufacturer and merchant, David Hesse, and, after its failure, returned to Ainsworth's Court to set up a more egalitarian New Synagogue under Hesse's presidency. The rebels included the stationer and tobacconist, David Missel, ancestor of the actor Warren Mitchell. The division was short-lived. The arrival in Manchester of a charismatic, learned and dynamic Hungarian Rabbi, Dr Solomon Schiller-Szinessy, an escapee from the Liberal Revolution of 1848, suggested the potential prestige of a reunion, while the arrival of an increasing number of immigrant paupers proved an increasing drain on the resources of a divided community. The division had been in no sense religious. It was about the nature of synagogue government and once the 'Free Members' had surrendered their privileged position, which they agreed to do in 1851, no further barriers to a harmonious reunion existed. On 18 January 1851 Schiller-Szinessy was installed as the minister of the two congregations, which were formally reunited the following April.

The Reform Movement

The results of a second rift in the Halliwell Street congregation were more permanent. In 1848 Manchester's Town Council announced that to build a major new road – to be called Corporation Street – giving improved access to the town centre, the Halliwell Street Synagogue would have to be compulsorily purchased and demolished. By chance, the announcement was followed in the early 1850s by a further split within the congregation, this one between those who wished to retain the traditional Jewish ritual and those who sought its modernisation. The 'modernisers' took their cue from the *Reform Movement*, which had already produced radical effects in Germany and London. The Reformers in London, through creating the West London Synagogue of British Jews in 1842, had initiated a programme of change which looked to simplify the synagogue ritual, to use English, in addition to Hebrew, as the language of prayer, and to additionally transform the layout of the synagogue so that the *Bimah*, the platform on which the reading desk stood, was moved from the centre of the building to the front, and to install an organ to accompany the synagogue choir. In terms of theology, while the traditionalists (otherwise the *Orthodox*) stood by the sanctity of the *Oral Law* (the traditional rabbinical interpretation of biblical texts), the Reformers believed that it needed to change in the light of intellectual and cultural advance in society at large. The problem this presented in Manchester was whether a new synagogue to replace Halliwell Street would follow traditional orthodox practice or move in the direction proposed by Reform.

In Manchester, the leadership of the Reform Movement was made up both of those who already had some experience of German Reform and those whose successful acculturation into Manchester society suggested to them that the synagogue, too, should become more English in style. The intellectual leader was the language teacher Tobias Theodores, a Berliner who in 1851 had become a lecturer in German at Owens College, out of which the University of Manchester was later to evolve. In 1842 Theodores had written a pamphlet, *The Oral Law and its Defenders*, in which he set out, in clear and dramatic form, what he saw as the philosophy of the Reform Movement. Most of those in Manchester who favoured his teaching were German-Jewish merchants in the textile trade, including Philip Lucas and his trading partner, Henry Micholls. Some of them also believed that the anglicisation of the synagogue service would assist the achievement of political emancipation. Set against them were most of Manchester's Jewish shopkeepers, many of them also German in origin but less integrated than their richer co-religionists into Manchester society, and the Jewish poor, reinforced from the mid-1840s by the arrival of the first immigrants, most of them manual workers or petty traders from

Architect's drawing of the intended Great Synagogue, 1856.

Rabbi Berendt Salomon in front of the Ark of the Great Synagogue c.1880.

Eastern Europe. The Eastern Europeans, in particular, hailed from parts of the German, Austrian and Russian empires in which Reform was unknown and Orthodox observance was central to daily life.

Much now depended on the stand which the new Rabbi, Solomon Schiller-Szinessy, chose to take. The fact that he favoured modernisation, while a majority of his congregants were intransigent in their opposition to change, ensured that the congregation would now divide permanently around the issue of Reform. Once the Halliwell Street Synagogue had been sold, the question became one of what manner of synagogue would replace it. Since neither party would yield ground, the money was placed at first in the Court of Chancery until some agreement was reached over its use. Finally the two parties, deciding that a compromise between them could not be achieved, divided the money between them and each went on to construct a synagogue to its own tastes. The Orthodox chose a site on land belonging to the Earl of Derby on Cheetham Hill Road. The Reformers, who in 1856 had formed themselves into a Reform Association with Schiller-Szinessy as their minister, opted for a site only half a mile away in Park Place, Cheetham. The Orthodox Great Synagogue, as it was later known, was consecrated on 11 March 1858; the Congregation of British Jews (otherwise the Reform Synagogue) three weeks later.

Both buildings were architecturally impressive. The Reform Synagogue was designed in a revived Gothic style by Edward Salomon, a local Jewish architect of growing prestige, who only a year earlier had designed the pavilion which had housed the Manchester Art Treasures Exhibition; while the Great was in the ornate, neo-Classical style of the municipal architect, Thomas Bird, sometimes described as 'Manchester Baroque'.

They marked a point in the history of the community at which the Jewish population had achieved the confidence to advertise, in a major middle-class and still largely Christian suburb, its sense of permanence. They were exercises in conspicuous display at a time when traditional hostility to the Jewish people was still a factor in Manchester life. One prestigious local Church of England Minister, Canon Hugh Stowell, had argued throughout the 1840s and early 1850s, with a strong

Interior of the Great Synagogue. (Courtesy Jewish Heritage UK and the Glyn family.)

and vocal following, that Jews had no right to a say in the government of a 'Christian country'. In fact, the movement for Jewish emancipation, supported by Manchester's Town Council, met with success. In 1845 municipal office was opened to Jews. Philip Lucas was unopposed when he stood as a Liberal for Cheetham Ward in 1851. In Manchester, 1858 marked a high point of Jewish confidence and it was also the point at which political emancipation was achieved nationally. By allowing Jewish MPs to avoid taking a Christian oath of allegiance, and with Baron Rothschild's entry to the House of Commons, Jews had become part of the government of Britain. The building of the two Manchester synagogues marked the local community's 'coming of age', both socially and politically.

The Manchester Congregation of British Jews, otherwise the Reform Synagogue, the first 'progressive' congregation in provincial Britain. (Courtesy Jewish Heritage UK and the Glyn family.)

While divided on matters of theology, liturgy and synagogue design, although even in these matters not as radically as their co-religionists in Berlin, the Reform and the Orthodox in Manchester were committed equally to the well-being and safety of the community. They had acted together in the movement for Jewish emancipation. In the years which followed, they co-operated without bitterness in the management of communal charities. Socially, however, they came to represent different sectors of the community. The Reform Congregation, the smaller of the two, was made up substantially of wealthier Manchester merchants engaged in the overseas trade, generally

Interior of the Reform Synagogue. (Courtesy Jewish Heritage UK and the Glyn family.)

with strong social and cultural connections with their Christian peers; while the Great Synagogue was essentially a congregation of shopkeepers, more numerous but also more remote from Manchester society. In the years which followed, communal institutions looked to the Reformers for their finances, their managers and for their links to what, in 1851, had become a city, and to the Great Synagogue for their religious inspiration. The relationship between them was generally friendly and occasionally close, as ministers were exchanged to provide sermons at Sabbath services. Some obtained membership of both synagogues. They were drawn together in part by the growth in the number of Eastern European immigrants, whose religious tastes and cultural baggage were unwelcome to the more anglicised Jews of German origin, whether committed to Reform or to Orthodoxy.

The creation of two major synagogues in Cheetham Hill also determined that it was north rather than south Manchester which would thereafter be the main centre of gravity of Manchester's Jewish population, with Cheetham Hill generally becoming known to Mancunians as 'the Jewish Quarter', 'Manchester's Palestine', and the south, where many Reformers had chosen to live, becoming better known for the mixing of its much smaller Jewish population with the native community. In more pejorative terms, south Manchester Jews were seen as more sophisticated and open in their cultural styles, whereas those in the north were seen as 'more Jewish' and inward-looking. To Jewish southerners, north Manchester was a ghetto; to Jewish northerners, south Manchester was seen as a step too close to assimilation. Reformers who lived as far south as Bowdon, in the Cheshire countryside, arrived at the Sabbath Services at the Reform Synagogue in horse-drawn carriages, while no Orthodox northerner would do other than walk to the synagogue on the Sabbath. Census records suggest that by 1858 the Jewish population of Manchester was nearing 2,000, and that Manchester Jewry had recently overtaken the communities in Liverpool and Birmingham to become the largest Jewish community in the British provinces.

Chapter 2

The Transformation of the Community, 1844–1875

The First Eastern Europeans

While the Jewish middle class in Manchester was consolidating its leadership of the community, active in the movement for political equality and raising the status of its divergent forms of Judaism, a new wave of immigrants was entering the town from Eastern Europe, particularly from the Russian Empire. The decisive factor in promoting their arrival was the opening of Manchester's Victoria Station in 1844, and so completing a relatively cheap route by rail and sea between the Russian Empire and Liverpool, the port of embarkation for the United States, to which a steerage passage cost only £3. Discriminatory legislation and compulsory military service (which typically involved the pressure to convert) had been causing concern to the Russo-Jewish population earlier; only in 1844 was it presented with a ready means of escape although, even then, this typically involved a clandestine crossing of the Russian border. Others, from East Prussia as well as Western Russia, saw escape by rail as a means of bettering themselves in the West, either in Britain or in the United States. Others again travelled westwards by boat from Russia's Baltic coast. Most were either manual workers or petty traders, while many others had no occupational experience of any kind and the vast majority arrived without material means.

Their arrival in Manchester, often only as transmigrants, is reflected in the records of a Joint Board of Relief set up in 1847 by the two competing synagogues, to give them a degree of support or to ease them on their journeys. Even then, they were seen in Manchester as a potential drain on minimal communal resources and as a threat to a community which, according to one of its members, 'had progressed alike in numbers, intelligence, wealth and all those qualities destined to raise men in the Social Scale'. The fear was that, with their lack of skills, their poverty, their foreign speech (Russian, Polish and

Libby Sheanaster in Russia, 1900. (Courtesy Manchester Jewish Museum.)

Menachem Kurchuk in Russia in 1905, prior to his emigration to Manchester. (Courtesy Manchester Jewish Museum.)

The Gottlieb family in Poland before their departure for Britain. (Courtesy Manchester Jewish Museum.)

Yiddish), their foreign dress and what were seen as their 'backward' religious customs, the newcomers would undermine the status that the Jewish middle class had achieved by their Englishness, their loyalty and their place within the Manchester bourgeoisie. Thus the community gave them no encouragement to remain, providing them with only minimal support for what was hoped to be a short stay in Manchester and occasionally raising the level of support to those who 'promised to leave town'. At one point a stone-yard was acquired by the community, in which newcomers were expected to work for their keep, in the hope that it would deter them

Typical travel document enabling a Jewish family to leave Russia in the 1890s.

from remaining. Meanwhile non-Jewish, chiefly German, merchants in Manchester established a Society for the Relief of Really Destitute and Deserving Foreigners which, like the Jewish Board of Relief, avoided any action which might encourage their poorer co-nationals to remain in the city. At one point the Board of Relief collaborated with the Society in persuading immigrants to return to Europe: if the Board covered their rail journey to Grimsby, the Society undertook to pay for their boat trip to Hamburg.

While such deterrent activities encouraged an unknown number of immigrants to either move on to Liverpool (where many were helped with a passage to the United States) or to return to the Continent, there were always those who, against the apparent odds, decided to remain in Manchester where jobs were available in the lowest ranks of the booming furniture and clothing trades and where the expectation was that, in the long run, the settled Jewish families, either from the imperative of charity which was part of Jewish teaching or to protect their own status, could be expected to offer a degree of charity or support. Since these were realistic expectations communicated by newcomers to their friends and relatives in Russia and the Polish-speaking districts of East Prussia, the flow of Eastern Europeans to Manchester gradually escalated, and while many of those subsequently disappointed left by choice for other British towns, for South Africa or (most commonly) for a United States in which the streets were paved with gold, many who achieved a modicum of success remained.

The Stern family in Odessa prior to their emigration. (Courtesy Manchester Jewish Museum.)

This was particularly true during the 1850s and 1860s as some of the religiously-inspired Eastern Europeans established **chevroth** (small religious societies which offered rudimentary facilities for religious worship, for socialising in Yiddish with their kinsmen, and for support in their initial survival) and the more enterprising of them set up tiny workshops, usually in their own homes, which manufactured clothing or furniture under contract

Eli Weitz, a shoemaker, with his family in Russia. (Courtesy Manchester Jewish Museum.)

with native shops and warehouses. While the chevroth offered intending settlers the kinds of religious services to which they had been accustomed in their home countries and the kinds of advice and support which might help them find work and accommodation, the domestic workshops held out the possibility of work with Jewish bosses likely to respect their kosher needs and religious observance, and particularly to provide time off to honour the Jewish Sabbath, which would have been

Bobbie Maysky who travelled from Lithuania to Manchester to attend her daughter's wedding in Cheetham Hill, c.1910. (Courtesy Manchester Jewish Museum.)

typically unavailable in any Christian workplace. The existence in many workshops of a subdivisional structure, by which each worker learnt only one of the processes of manufacture, also leant itself to the employment of immigrants who arrived with few or no industrial skills. To those unable to find work at first, a chevra might offer cheap goods, like sponges, wash-leathers or, in one instance, 'two pounds of rhubarb', with a ready market on the streets of Manchester, a glazier's diamond with which an immigrant might earn a living as a mender of windows, or a sewing machine to make clothing at home for one or other of the workshop masters.

A Voluntary Ghetto

The consequence was the gradual construction of what has been called a 'voluntary ghetto': an area of residence in which cheap (and usually overcrowded) accommodation was available, Jewish shops and workshops proliferated, and immigrant chevroth were thick on the ground. Such an area was Red Bank, a sandstone ridge of jerry-built property (its streets held up by fragile retaining walls), industrial pollution and civic neglect, which lay between the homes of Jewish middle-class families in Cheetham Hill and the railway and River Irk (then an open sewer) at the city end of Cheetham Hill Road. It was thus an area of immigrant self-help, yet close enough to settled Jewish families, from whom a degree of charity might be expected, and to the Great Synagogue which offered free seating for the High Festivals, with which the chevroth were ill-equipped to deal. In the chevroth the immigrants found, for only a penny or twopence a week, the kind of informal services with long discourses in Yiddish that were not available in the staid Great Synagogue, with

New emigrants from Eastern Europe in Manchester, the Silverman family. (Courtesy Manchester Jewish Museum.)

its costly membership fees and church-like decorum. In contrast, the chevroth were often no more than two back-yards covered with metal sheeting, a back room or an attic. They had names which either symbolised their religiosity (one was the Chevra *Torah* – the Society of the Holy Law) or the source of their original members (the Polish Chevra, the Cracow Chevra or the Chevra Walkawishk). By the early 1860s, the number of chevroth in Red Bank had risen to around 15 and

Tailors' workshop on Cheetham Hill Road, c.1910. (Courtesy Manchester Jewish Museum.)

the Jewish population was nearing 4,000, of whom, perhaps, 700 were Eastern Europeans, most of them living, working and worshipping in or near Red Bank.

Since the immigrant workshops competed among themselves, as well as with Christian factories, for contracts to supply clothing or furniture to high-street shops or trade warehouses at the cheapest rates, working hours were long (up to 16 hours a day), wages were minimal and working conditions were poor (and frequently unsafe and unhealthy). The very existence of immigrant workshops was fragile and bankruptcies were common, with aspiring workshop masters being, not uncommonly, forced to return to the shop floor. In most, work outside a family group was available only in the 'busy seasons', with most workers sacked without mercy as the 'slack' season set in. In the long term, competition also gave rise to the survival of only those most equipped with skill, managerial competence or capital resources. Some of these went on to create purpose-built factories, particularly for the manufacture of cheap furniture and clothing, cloth caps or waterproof garments, while most 'sweatshops', some after sparking briefly, disappeared without trace. While expensive waterproof clothing had been made in Manchester by Charles Mackintosh since the early 19th century, the

Group of workers from Flacks tailoring workshop in Salford, c.1910. (Courtesy Manchester Jewish Museum.)

Samuel Sasupskie's shop in Openshaw, East Manchester. Sasupskie, an immigrant glazier, had the idea of locating his business near the engineering plants of east Manchester, with their constant need for window replacements. (Courtesy Manchester Jewish Museum.)

manufacture of cheap waterproofs, made possible by the near simultaneous invention of the sewing machine and of cheaper methods of vulcanising india-rubber, was an invention of Jewish immigrants. These immigrants were chiefly members of a closely connected network of Cracower families who, in 1859, created the Cracow Chevra in Robert Street, Cheetham, just beyond the edge of Red Bank.

In 1875, when the number of Eastern Europeans had probably reached 3,000, perhaps half the total Jewish population, they were still too hidden away in such inaccessible slums as Red Bank, in exclusively Jewish workshops and in chevroth barely visible to the human eye, to attract the hostile attention of the Christian public. They formed a close-knit community which no Christian had any need to enter. They did not yet impinge on the 'respectable' residential districts of the Christian population. The impact on Jewish Manchester, however, was altogether different. Whether as co-religionists in need of costly care and attention, as a stain on the landscape of British-Jewish respectability,

Interior of a bake house in Red Bank owned by the Russian immigrant, Bernard Baker. (Courtesy Manchester Jewish Museum.)

or as the promoters of a style of Judaism at odds with that of the settled community and advocated by increasingly vocal and ambitious immigrant rabbis, they could not be ignored. By the late 1870s the more upwardly mobile had begun to make their way into what, until then, had been an attractive middle-class suburb. They were perceived as 'bringing down' the quality of life for those long settled, anglicising Jewish families in the lower parts of Cheetham Hill.

The Jewish Board of Guardians

One result of the growth of a vulnerable Jewish working class of Eastern European origin was the evolution of the 1840s makeshift Board of Relief into a highly organised Jewish Board of Guardians, based in part on the Board of Guardians of the city of Manchester, and in part on the Jewish Board of Guardians set up in London in 1859, itself modelled on British forms of public relief. In its origins in 1867, the Board owed little to traditional notions of Jewish charity. It was seen, essentially, at least at first, as a mechanism created by middle-class Jews to resolve a problem rather than to meet

a need. To avoid it being, or being seen as, an institution which would attract further Jewish immigration, it offered only one financial payment during the first six months of an immigrant's life in Manchester: an incentive too, it was supposed, for their departure. Applications for relief were thoroughly investigated by a Board, the leading members of which were members of the Reform Synagogue (while most of the poor were Orthodox), to ensure, in the manner of British public charity, that the applicant was 'deserving'. The Board set itself against the idea of

a 'dependent' class. The object was to tide the immigrants over and lend them support (with equipment, interest-free loans or apprenticeships) until they were in a position to help themselves, or perhaps decided to depart. It was also used as a means of cultural control. No immigrant parents were to receive help until they had agreed to send their children to the Jews' School and to give up their membership of what were described as 'clandestine societies' (that is, the chevroth).

Restaurant at 15 Park Street, Cheetham Hill, c.1905.

Cheetham Town Hall, built during 1853–56 as the administrative centre of Cheetham Hill, then a separate township. When Cheetham Hill was incorporated into the city of Manchester, it became the Cheetham Public Hall and, because of its position, an important venue for Jewish events. (Courtesy Mr Merton Paul.)

First offices of the
Manchester Jewish
Board of Guardians,
Knowsley Street,
Manchester,
photographed c.1900.
The offices of the board
were moved in 1919 to a
house on Cheetham Hill
Road donated by the
industrialist Isidore
Frankenburg. (Courtesy
Jewish Heritage UK and
the Glyn family.)

The Manchester Jews'
School in Derby Street,
opened in 1869.
(Courtesy Jewish
Heritage UK and the
Glyn family.)

The Board, apart from being a 'deterrent charity', was also part of a strategic attack deployed by an anglicised Jewish elite, who had set the Board up and controlled its workings, on Yiddish as a language and Eastern European styles as an appropriate expression of British Judaism. Both were seen as dangers to the status of the established Jewish middle class and perhaps to the good image, and thus the safety, of the community. It reflected the wide cultural gulf between a well-to-do Jewish middle class of German, Dutch or Sephardi origin and an Eastern European working class. The Jews' School was moved in 1869, in the light of its expanding intake, to purpose-built premises in Derby Street, Cheetham. It was attended chiefly by the children of immigrant families, over 700 in all, but, by 1875, the managers of the school set their face against what they saw as a 'foreign patois'. The speaking of Yiddish at the school was an offence. Children arriving at the school with Yiddish first names (for example Tauba, the Yiddish for 'dove') stood the risk of having them changed to respectable English first names. Tauba herself, a very real person, became Matilda. Parents who applied for garments for their children to the Jews' School Clothing Society received help only if they were judged by its anglicised managers to be 'respectable'.

An immense social distance separated a Jewish commercial plutocracy from the foreign poor, one of whose evocative addresses was 'Number 3 in the Cellar, Back Fernie Street, Red Bank'. In 1875 there were two Jewish homes in Manchester with 24 residents. One was a terraced house in Red Bank housing three immigrant families and 12 lodgers, all engaged in the lower levels of the tailoring industry, the other was a home in south Manchester of Edward Behrens, an export merchant, with a family of five and 19 servants, all of them non-Jewish and including a coachman and under coachman. While most of the Eastern Europeans struggled to survive, batteries of English Irish, Scots and Welsh servants serviced the Jewish middle classes. During the 1860s and 1870s, however, a small number of enterprising Eastern Europeans had begun to translate their domestic workshops into small factories and develop middle-class aspirations themselves. Known to the Yiddish press as the *alrightniks*, they began to seek a status in the community which reflected their (at first modest) economic success.

The South Manchester Synagogue

Such status-seeking included an ambition for membership of the Great Synagogue, so dominated by established families as to be known as the 'Englischer *Schule*' (the English Synagogue). The struggle which ensued, as immigrants were at first blackballed by the existing members and subsequently forced their way in, had dire consequences for what had, up to then, been the solidarity Orthodox Jewry, at least among the middle classes. In the late 1860s, some 20 members of the Great Synagogue, chiefly among the more successful and most anglicised city shopkeepers, began a movement to create the first Orthodox synagogue in south Manchester, after being distressed by, in their view, the distasteful arguments which increasingly marked general meetings, and the already ill-at-ease atmosphere in Cheetham Hill, which they now shared with unsophisticated Yiddish-speaking 'foreigners'. Some had already moved their homes to the area of Chorlton-on-Medlock, a middle-class residential district in south Manchester, and now sought to create a synagogue within walking distance; most were still living in Cheetham Hill and required a synagogue in the south which would justify their resettlement. The result, in 1872, was first the holding of services in rented premises in the Chorlton-on-Medlock district of the city, including Chorlton Town Hall, and then the conversion of houses in Sidney Street, All Saints, into the South Manchester Synagogue, with an initial membership of 40. The synagogue was consecrated by the Chief Rabbi on 17 September 1873.

The South Manchester Synagogue in All Saints, 1873. The congregation moved to new premises in Wilbraham Road, Fallowfield, in 1913. (Courtesy Jewish Heritage UK and the Glyn family.)

Invitation to the consecration of the South Manchester Synagogue in Sidney Street, All Saints, 17 September 1873.

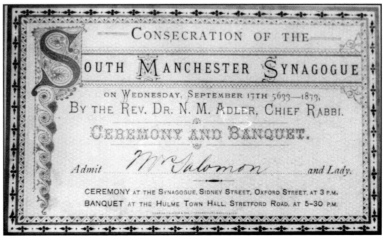

Interior of the South Manchester Synagogue in All Saints, 1873. (Courtesy Jewish Heritage UK and the Glyn family.)

Deciding on what they described as 'gentle reform' – a reform, that is, of the aesthetics of the synagogue rather than the content of Judaism or the form of the ritual – the dissenters, using a former second minister of the Great Synagogue as their religious leader, had created what was, in effect, a synagogue based on snobbery. They were in retreat from an increasingly densely packed Jewish Quarter, in which the Eastern European sector was expanding with increasing rapidity, and in which uppity Eastern European alrightniks threatened to disturb the quiet and undermine the respectability of their synagogue.

The Spanish and Portuguese Synagogue

In that same Great Synagogue were well-to-do Sephardi merchants from Aleppo, Cairo, Gibraltar and other ports on the Mediterranean coast, who, in the absence of a place of worship reflecting the religious and cultural specifics of the Sephardi heritage, had chosen membership of the only prestigious Orthodox congregation in town. They too, while not personally involved, were uneasy witnesses to the storms generated in the Great Synagogue by congregational tensions. For them also, chiefly living in the upper regions of Cheetham Hill, an area not yet reached by Eastern European settlers, decision time, long delayed, had arrived. A few individuals chose to join the founders of the South Manchester Synagogue, while others created private Sephardi minyanim, first in private houses, then in the former premises of the Jews' School at 78 Cheetham Hill Road. During 1872–73, the heads of some 20 Sephardi families, all of them engaged in the overseas trade, took the first steps towards the creation of a Sephardi Synagogue in Manchester. They employed the now highly regarded Jewish architect, Edward Salomon, to create a place of worship appropriate to their historical experience. Employing what he described as a 'Saracenic' (that is, Muslim) style which had been used for the design of synagogues in mediaeval Spain, and later in the Mediterranean countries of Sephardi resettlement, Salomon created the Manchester Spanish and Portuguese Synagogue (now the Manchester Jewish Museum) on Cheetham Hill Road, which opened on 6 May 1874. The synagogue, under the presidency of the leading cotton textile exporter Isaac David Belisha (grandfather of the politician Leslie Hore Belisha), accepted the prayer book and usages of Bevis Marks, the

The Spanish and Portuguese Synagogue, 1874. (Courtesy Jewish Heritage UK and the Glyn family.)

London Sephardi congregation dating from 1701, and placed itself under the religious jurisdiction of the Haham, the Sephardi equivalent of the Chief Rabbi.

Among the more colourful of the founder members was Moses Joseph Bianco, born in Syria in 1848, who founded an export firm with its warehouse in Bootle Street. Not too successful as a cotton merchant, at the rear of his warehouse, which backed onto Peter Street, he created a small coffee shop which became an informal meeting place for Sephardi traders, who sealed business deals over coffee and cigars. This, in turn, grew into a successful restaurant, the Café Royal, named after the famous Theatre Royal on the opposite side of Peter Street. Next to the café, Bianco opened a tobacconist which, among other things, sold an imported cigar made to his own specifications and named the Flor de Bianco. More typically, Sephardi merchants working in central Manchester from warehouses, some of them palatial, extended the market for Manchester textiles into South America, the Mediterranean coastlands and the Far East.

Interior of the Spanish and Portuguese Synagogue, 1874. (Courtesy Jewish Heritage UK and the Glyn family.)

Ark of the Spanish and Portuguese Synagogue, decorated for a Jewish Festival. (Courtesy Manchester Jewish Museum.)

Street Scene in Red Bank. (Courtesy Manchester Jewish Museum.)

Red Bank and the Chevroth

The foundation of the Spanish and Portuguese Synagogue added the final piece to a mosaic of 'major' synagogues which, between them, until the late 1880s, catered for every social, religious and cultural segment of a middle-class Jewry. Only the Eastern Europeans lacked a prestigious place of worship to embody their own religious styles, their needs met only by a galaxy of chevroth, many of them transient, changing their locations and names in response to a poor but dynamic Eastern European working class. William Aronsberg, an immigrant optician of the 1840s from Courland on the Baltic coast of Russia was, by the 1870s, a man of substance, prominent in city philanthropy. Aronsberg made an ambitious attempt to draw the chevroth together into a shared synagogue and *Beth Hamedrash* (House of Study). His failure probably had as much to do with fissures in the world of the chevroth, perhaps 20 in number by 1874, as with the tendency of their leading members to seek an improved status by abandoning their Eastern European heritage, diluting the strength of their observance and moving, via the Great Synagogue, into the religious and social world of the Jewish middle classes. The Eastern European poor, perhaps half the total Jewish population of 10,000 by 1875, spilled over into other districts, into former middle-class homes in the lower reaches of Cheetham, into large but decaying property in Strangeways and into the working class terraces of Lower Broughton, across the Irwell in Salford – taking with them their chevroth and their workshops. In 1877, since they lacked the right to burial in the cemeteries of the major synagogues, a group of minor businessmen of Eastern European origin created the 'Manchester Burial Society of Polish Jews Limited', which granted the right of its shareholders to interment in a burial ground acquired by the society in Urmston.

Street Scene in Red Bank. (Courtesy Manchester Jewish Museum.)

Although the major synagogues of the Jewish middle classes became obvious symbols of the Jewish presence, few of the developments within the Eastern European and working-class sector of the Manchester community were at first visible to the non-Jewish population of Manchester. To the native Manchester population, these Jewish working-class communities, forming an inner circle of slums around Manchester and Salford, were the city's 'immigrant districts', into which they rarely ventured. An exception was the journalist Walter Tomlinson, who in his *Bye-Ways of Manchester Life*, published in 1887, included the first brief (and jaundiced) account of the Jewish residents of Red Bank. 'If they have godliness', Tomlinson wrote, 'most decidedly they have not cleanliness. We walked through Fernie Street [Red Bank] one evening lately. The houses literally boiled over with people, grown persons and children, to such an extent that one could only walk up the middle of the street. The feeling we carried away was that we should have liked them much better if they had looked more wholesome.' More generally, Tomlinson was modestly sympathetic towards Manchester Jews. 'They are still a peculiar people,' he wrote, 'with us but not of us…and we know so little of his ways and practices, his merits and demerits, that we are still too much inclined in the main to look upon the Jew simply as a spoiler of the Gentiles.'

Chapter 3

'The Alien Question'
1875–1914

Immigration from the Russian Empire increased, especially after the assassination of Tsar Alexander in 1881. Blamed on Jewish anarchists, one of whom had certainly been involved, the assassination led to violent public attacks on Jewish homes, which the Government did little to curtail, and which were followed by legislation (the infamous 'May Laws') further restricting the occupational and residential rights of Russian Jewry. Some left Russia from the centres of violence, others, members of radical socialist groups, to escape arrest. Most sought to surmount the poverty that their limited rights entailed and which were exacerbated by changes in the Russian economy, which were rendering the traditional handcrafts of the Jewish worker increasingly obsolete. From 1901 an increasing number of Jews left Romania in the face of popular and governmental anti-Semitism. The destination of most Eastern Europeans, encouraged by committees in towns across Europe including Manchester and Liverpool, was the 'Golden Medina' of the United States, where Jewish immigrants transformed the cities of the Eastern seaboard. Others made their way to London's East End or dropped off along the main route of transmigration, creating or expanding a chain of Jewish communities across the north of Britain which included Hull,

Jacob Doniger's Cap Factory, 'The Clarence Hat Works', in Julia Street, Cheetham. With three factories in Cheetham, Doniger, a Russian immigrant, was the leading Manchester manufacturer of cloth caps. (Courtesy Mr Merton Paul.)

Leeds, Middlesbrough, Sunderland and (primarily) Manchester. By 1905 immigrants from Eastern Europe constituted perhaps three quarters of a Manchester Jewish population of around 25,000; by 1914 perhaps four-fifths, or more, of a community of 30,000.

Communal Tension

The last quarter of the 19th century was characterised by tension and occasional conflict between an 'old' community, chiefly of German, Dutch and Sephardi origin, who were declining in numbers but clinging to communal power, and a growing 'new' community of Eastern Europeans and their children. This was only partly a conflict between rich and poor since, although the majority of the Eastern Europeans were manual workers and petty traders, by the 1880s a handful of the more skilled and enterprising had created major industries in the clothing and furniture trades. It was also a conflict between two ways of being Jewish in the Manchester Diaspora. For members of the 'old' community, the emphasis was on cultural integration; for members of the 'new', on the preservation of the religious values they had brought with them from Eastern Europe. Nor was the conflict either lost or won. More typically it resulted in compromises between the religiosity of the newcomers and the assimilationist tendencies of the long established. It was out of a concoction of such compromises, and against a background of Christian hostility to the Jewish 'alien', that a 'modern' community had evolved by 1914.

The furriers shop and workshop at 81 Cheetham Hill Road of the Russian immigrant, Simon Blaiwais, seen here in the doorway. The small-scale manufacture of fur coats was another trade entered by immigrants from Eastern Europe. (Courtesy Manchester Jewish Museum.)

Anti-alienism

The response to the immigrants in Christian Manchester was to increasingly hold them responsible for Manchester's late 19th century 'ills': growing unemployment, worker unrest, a shortage of housing, the increasing cost of poverty and the social decline of suburban areas closest to the city centre. In effect, Jewish immigrants became the scapegoats for working and living conditions for which they were, at most, only peripherally responsible, and which were more obviously the consequence of economic crisis, the expansion of the consumer market and urban development.

In Manchester a sustained verbal assault on 'alien invaders', most of them Jewish, began in 1887 with the first calls for a restriction on 'pauper immigration'. The weekly newspaper, the *Manchester City News*, led the way. It was an anomaly, the *City News* claimed in April 1887, to promote emigration as a means of limiting local poverty, while encouraging 'by the freedom of our immigration laws the settlement in our towns of European

TOP LEFT: Joinery shop of the Pollick family in Great Ducie Street, Strangeways, 1907. Joinery (rather than cabinet-making) was a rare occupation for Eastern European immigrants. The Pollicks lived in the Cheetwood area of Cheetham Hill. (Courtesy Manchester Jewish Museum.)

TOP RIGHT: Rosenberg's butcher's shop at 133 Bury New Road, established in 1895. (Courtesy Manchester Jewish Museum.)

BOTTOM LEFT: The Magnet Bakery established by the Sieff family at the corner of Broughton Street and Cheetham Hill Road. (Copyright Manchester Central Library.)

BOTTOM RIGHT: David Hollstein outside his gents rainwear factory, Hollstein and Portnoy, c.1920. (Courtesy Manchester Jewish Museum.)

paupers'. The attack broadened in April 1888 when an enquiry conducted by the medical journal, the *Lancet*, into the sweated industries of Manchester and Liverpool, revealed that sweating, which had earlier attracted adverse comment only in the East End of London, was equally prevalent in the north of England. Manchester, the report concluded, was 'completely honeycombed by sweaters'. Out of a total of 5,000 persons employed in the tailoring trade in the city, 1,300 were said to be 'sweated', either in small workshops or as home workers. Pay was low, hours long, the workplaces overcrowded, dilapidated, 'deplorably dirty…hot and malodorous'. *The Lancet* went on to identify 'Jew sweaters' as the chief perpetrators of such evils and Strangeways as the main site of their operations. It was immigrants, too, in the *Lancet's* view, who were introducing into Manchester 'dirty habits foreign to our ideas of salubrity'.

The revelations of the *Lancet* opened the way for a virulent anti-alienism in which spokesmen for such public institutions as the Poor Law Unions, the Factory Inspectorate and the Chamber of Commerce were aided and abetted by trade unionists, local councillors and the local press. Only the *Manchester Guardian* held aloof from such slanderous muck-raking. The immigrants were

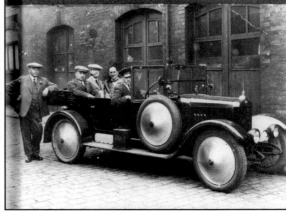

variously described as 'the scum and residuum of humanity' and 'shoals of stunted paupers'. Decent native suburbs were being turned into 'foreign enclaves', insular, 'cheerless' and 'intensely and disagreeably dirty'. The native inhabitants were 'in flight' as the newcomers turned respectable property into 'filthy dens' and decent and orderly provision stores into unhygienic nightmares, their meat consisting 'mostly of flies', the fish piled up on the pavements 'quite low enough for any stray cat or dog to reach without trouble', rows of bottles 'in all stages of uncleanliness', the shelving 'unlined and unwashed'. Such refined native suburban pastimes as bowls and cricket were being undermined, it was said, by the barbarous outsiders. Native workers, displaced by foreigners, were increasing the burden on the rates. The Jewish immigrant was depicted as a 'carrier' of dirt, disease, un-English

TOP LEFT: Joel Wallman's second-hand furniture shop in Waterloo Road, 1912. (Courtesy Manchester Jewish Museum.)

TOP RIGHT: Cheetham Village, c.1905. (Copyright Manchester Central Library.)

Front page of an issue of The Jewish Record, *a Manchester Jewish newspaper hostile to 'alien immigrants,' which survived for only three months.*

customs, and the 'dismal doctrines' of continental socialism. He competed 'unfairly' for work and housing, so lowering wages and increasing rents. He was typically 'gaunt-eyed', 'unhealthy and undersized'; his wife, weighed down by jewellery, and dressed in tastelessly garish clothes, was 'unlovely' especially in her 'dark and ugly wig'. Such repetitive comment was often framed in anti-semitic imagery. Even within the working-class immigrant districts, 'chicanery and greed for gain' were said to predominate, 'as they did of old'. The 'only object was money-getting' and children were encouraged to 'talk of bargains when other children talk of toys'. Education was seen 'solely…as an avenue to a small business'. In April 1891 a local journalist, Henry Yeo, published the first edition of a new

*Cartoon from the
Manchester anti-alien
monthly,* Spy, *suggesting
the threat supposedly
posed to native tailors by
Jewish immigrants.*

journal, *Spy*, the pages of which were suffused with crude anti-Semitism and fierce xenophobia. Yeo combined typical attacks on aliens as the inventors of sweating and as unscrupulous competitors for jobs and houses, with a physical attack on Jews which anticipated Nazi propaganda. To Yeo, Jews 'were just as desireable as rats', they were 'refuse', 'pests', 'vermin', 'insectoria', 'Yids' and 'smogs'. In a supposedly comic piece entitled '*the Oppressed become the Oppressors*', complete with a cartoon and a poem, he sought to show how the victim of Russian oppression turned inevitably into the 'grasping' Jew of the Manchester streets. The poem ends:

> *How do they show their gratitude?*
> *Why, in the old sweet way,*
> *The Opresss'd ones turn oppressors,*
> *And show the cloven heel,*
> *The life-blood squeezing from our men,*
> *Our female's virtues steal.*

For Yeo the sweated immigrant tailor, while displacing native workers, was simply 'saving where others would starve' against the day when he emerged

*Anti-Semitic cartoon
from* Spy *illustrating a
poem entitled '*The
Oppressed become the
Oppressors.' *On the left,
a persecuted Russian
Jewish peasant; on the
right, a Jewish
pawnbroker in
Manchester.*

*Lewin Hats Limited, a
cap-making factory in
Robert Street,
Cheetham. (Copyright
Manchester Central
Library.)*

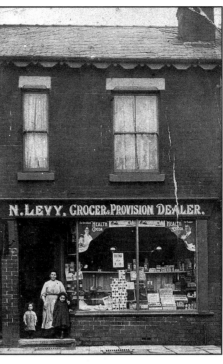

TOP LEFT: Morris Levy's Manchester furniture shop, established in 1873. (Courtesy Manchester Jewish Museum.)

Mr N. Levy's grocery in St James Street, Salford. (Courtesy Manchester Jewish Museum.)

himself as an exploiting sweater. Claiming 20,000 readers, Yeo continued to publish *Spy* until successful libel actions, at least one of them mounted by a local Jewish trader, Moses Besso, led to his bankruptcy and incarceration as a 'criminal lunatic' in Prestwich Asylum in 1899.

In the more muted versions of the attack, the immigrants were conceded their 'good points'. They were hard-working, they drank 'in moderation or not at all', they loved their families, and they were 'very religious'. Their children were slowly learning English ways. But they were 'increasing too rapidly' and steps should be taken to keep their brothers and sisters 'outside the country'.

For all the invective of *Spy*, anti-alienism and anti-Semitism were probably less intense in Manchester than in the East End of London. The Jewish aliens had their Manchester allies, not least C.P. Scott, the powerful editor of the *Manchester Guardian*, and the influential heads of Manchester's two major secondary schools, Manchester Grammar School (J.L. Paton) and Manchester High School for Girls (Sara Burstall). Unlike London, Manchester produced no coherent or influential party or pressure group urging on the Government the restriction of alien immigration. Although themselves not welcoming the arrival of Jewish paupers, some well-to-do Jews of Eastern European origin were active in condemning the assault on their poorer co-religionists.

The Greengate and Irwell Rubber Company, a firm established in the 1860s by the Russian immigrant Isidore Frankenburg for the manufacture of rubber, leather and waterproof goods. It was Frankenburg's boast at the time of the Alien Question that he employed 'only British labour'. (Courtesy Manchester Jewish Museum.)

Nationally, however, after convening a Royal Commission on Alien Immigration, which discovered, *inter alia*, that sweating was not an 'alien invention', a Conservative Government was persuaded to appease the anti-aliens by introducing an Aliens Act which, in 1905, placed restrictions on foreign immigration. Although relatively mild in its provisions – it excluded only those 'undesirables' who lacked an adequate means of support, had criminal records or suffered from infectious diseases – and administered by a Liberal Government which came to power in 1906, the Aliens Act provided the platform on which all future immigration restrictions in Britain were based. It also appeared to satisfy public opinion on the 'Alien Question'. Vocal anti-alien feeling in Manchester was all but silenced as the Government turned to legislative means of curbing the excesses of the workshop trades. The cost was that the Act appeared to give a degree of validity to the notion of an 'undesirable' foreigner embedded in anti-alien propaganda.

The Alrightniks

The irony was that, while *Spy* and its lesser contemporaries reviled the new immigrants as a force subversive of the Manchester economy, the reality was that the more successful among them were creating firms which were contributing to the city's prosperity. The mass production of cheap waterproof garments was a Jewish immigrant invention. Through immigrant enterprise Manchester had, by the 1890s, become the home of major factories manufacturing cloth caps and waterproof clothing. An inscription still to be found above the

Wolf Marks with the staff of his tailoring workshop in Cannon Street, Manchester, 1904. (Courtesy Manchester Jewish Museum.)

entrance to one late 19th-century factory in Derby Street, Cheetham Hill – 'The Anchor Cap Works. Nathan Hope. Founded 1853' – suggests the way in which an early immigrant from Russia, Nathan Hope, having first created a domestic workshop in his home (in 1853) had, by the 1890s, prospered sufficiently to build a substantial cap-making factory employing over 500 workers.

The Russian immigrant, Lazar Atlas, outside his fruit shop in Cheetham Hill, 1912. (Courtesy Manchester Jewish Museum.)

Members of the Russian immigrant Doniger family progressed from establishing a domestic workshop in 1863 to the ownership of two major factories by 1896 (the Clarence and Empire Cap Works), which produced more cloth caps than any other firm in Britain. The factories of Cohen and Wilks and Levy and Weisgard, also in Derby Street, were among Britain's largest firms producing waterproof clothing.

Immigrants also brought new forms of retail trading to the city. In 1880 David Lewis (formerly Levy), once an apprentice to Benjamin Hyam and whose first clothing shops had been in Liverpool, opened his first Manchester 'multiple store' in Market Street. This 'People's Emporium', with its wide range of goods, cheap prices and extravagant advertising, both attracted the Manchester public

and shocked established shopkeepers accustomed to more subdued methods of marketing their goods. Among those arriving in Britain from the Russian Empire in 1882 was the young Michael Marks, who, after first trading as a pedlar on the streets of Leeds, opened a series of market stalls characterised

Sales floor of Marks and Spencer's shop in Oldham Street, 1925. (Courtesy Manchester Jewish Museum.)

*Marks and Spencer
Penny Bazaar in
Oldham Street,
Manchester, opened in
March 1896. (Courtesy
Manchester Jewish
Museum.)*

*The first Marks and
Spencer Warehouse and
Central Offices, built in
Derby Street, Cheetham,
between 1899 and 1901.
(Courtesy Mr Merton
Paul.)*

by the phrase 'Don't ask the price, it's a penny',
and thus known as 'Penny Bazaars'. In 1894
Marks settled in Manchester, where he entered
into partnership with Tom Spencer, a former
clerk at the Leeds warehouse from which he had
obtained his goods, to create Marks and
Spencer. His first shop, as distinct from market
stall, was opened in the same year on Cheetham
Hill Road where he himself first lived. In 1899
building work began in Derby Street for the
construction of the firm's first head offices and
warehouse, opened in 1901. It was only in the
early 1920s, after the firm had achieved
spectacular success with its base in Manchester, that the company removed its
headquarters to London's Baker Street. After Marks's early death in 1908, and
a brief struggle for succession, the firm passed into the hands of his son, Simon,
and son-in-law, Israel Sieff.

Chapter 4

The Socialist and Trade Union Tradition

In public attacks on the 'alien', the Jewish immigrant was not only held responsible for the creation of sweating but was often said to have favoured it, as a system in which, through saving 'where an Englishman would starve', he might himself attain entrepreneurial status as the 'master' of a workshop.

In this way, he would satisfy what were described as his 'entrepreneurial tastes'. While it is true that most Jewish workers found no way of advancement in the immigrant trades other than to become a master, the notion of 'entrepreneurial tastes' is best seen as another evocation of the anti-Semitic 'Shylock image'. In the real world, the Jewish immigrant was as anxious to improve his pay and working conditions as his critics were to eliminate sweating. What he lacked at first was the means and the ideology which might

רולס.

1) דער נאמען פון קלוב איז: „דער מאנטשעסטער אינ-טערנאציאנאלער ארבייטער בילדונגס קלוב".

2) דער צוועק פון קלוב איז: צו בילדען און אויפקלערען דיא ארבייטער דורך פארטרעגע און א לעזע-צימער, און אלע וויכטיגע און ניצליכע פראגען, וואס זיינען פערבונדען מיט זייער היינטיגע שלעכטע לאגע, און וויא אזוי זיי קענען ברייננען פאר זיך א זיכערען און א גליקליכען לעבען: צו פעראייניגען דיא ארבייטער פון דיא פערשידענע מלאכות און זיי וויא ווייט מעגליך צו שיצען געגען זייערע סוועטערס: אויך צו אונטער-האלטען דיא מיטגליעדער דורך קאנצערטע, דראמאטישע פארשטעלונגען א. ז. וו.

3) יעדער ארבייטער, מאן אדער פרוי, וואס שטימט איין מיט דיא פרינציפען פון קלוב און פערפפליכטעט זיך דיזעלבע צו אונטערשטיצען, קען ווערן א מעמבער. א קאנדידאט מוז פארגעשלאגען ווערן פון א מעמבער און ווערט ערוועהלט ביי דיא נעכסטע מעמבערס-פערזאמלונג. א מאנספערזאן-מעמבער צאהלט 9 פענס ביים איינשרייבען און 3 פענס וועכענטליך; א פרויענצימער-מעמבער צאהלט פ. און 2 פ.

4) אלע קלוב-אנגעלעגנהייטען ווערען געפיהרט פון א קאמיטע, וועלכע בעשטייט פון א סעקרעטער, א קאסירער, דריי טרוסטיס, א ביבליאטהעקאר, א סטיידושו מענעדשער, א דאאר-מאן און צוויי באר-סטיואדס. דאס קאמיטע ווערט געוועהלט אלע 3 מאנאט ביי דיא גענעראל-פערזאמלונג: א

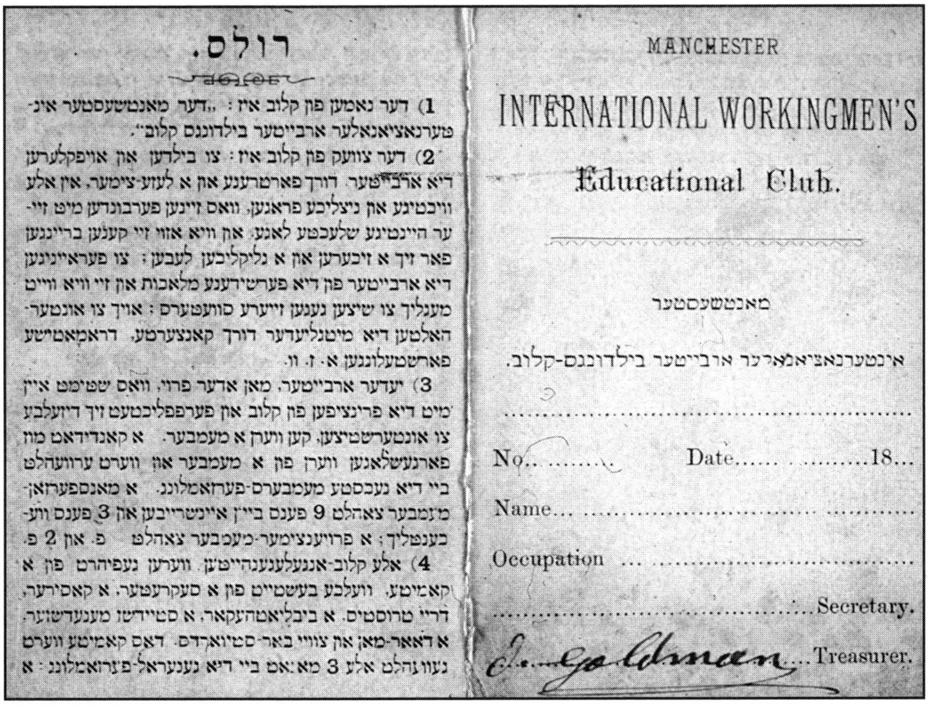

MANCHESTER

INTERNATIONAL WORKINGMEN'S

Educational Club.

מאנטשעסטער

אינטערנאציאנאלער ארבייטער בילדונגס-קלוב.

....

No.............. Date.................18...

Name..

Occupation ....

.....................................Secretary.

J. Goldman ... Treasurer.

Membership Card of the International Working Men's club, Manchester, 1889.

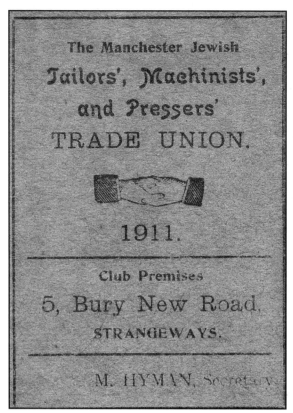

The Manchester Jewish
Tailors', Machinists',
and Pressers'
TRADE UNION.

1911.

Club Premises
5, Bury New Road,
STRANGEWAYS.

M. HYMAN, Secretary

Membership card of Harry Cohen of the Jewish Tailors', Machinists', and Pressers' Trade Union, 1911. Harry Cohen was born in Riga and arrived in Manchester with his parents when he was six months old. He settled in Strangeways and entered the tailoring trade. He was occasionally sacked by the masters of garment workshops for 'disrupting the workers.' (Courtesy Manchester Jewish Museum.)

have helped him to achieve it. Before 1888 he resisted exploitation largely by the inadequate means of court action against his employer. Once he had made contact with Britain's Trade Union tradition, he used it to great effect. For their part, English trade unionists were anxious to persuade the immigrants to enter the field of collective bargaining, if only to prevent the erosion of their own bargaining power. Encouraging the Jewish worker was the public agitation which depicted sweating as an unacceptable part of the British economy and which accused the Jewish worker of having created it.

Jewish trade unionism in Manchester thus evolved in the late 1880s, as Jewish workers in the city's clothing workshops were brought into contact with the radical 'new unionism' that was evolving within the unskilled sectors of the English workforce. This was largely through the example and personal mediation of Jewish trade unionists and socialists from London and Leeds, where Jewish workers had been active in the Socialist movement since the 1870s and in Trade Unionism since 1884–5.

Jewish Socialism

It would seem that Socialism entered Jewish Manchester in 1889 through links between a handful of (unnamed) immigrant Jewish socialists settled in Manchester, and Wilhelm (born Woolf) Wess, an immigrant to London of Lithuanian origin, a member of the British Socialist League, and the International Workingmen's Educational Club (IWEC), which had been set up by Jewish workers and intellectuals at 40 Berner Street in London's East End in February 1885. In January 1889 Wess was in Manchester to help establish a Manchester IWEC, probably in Strangeways. Its aims (printed in Yiddish on the reverse of membership cards) were the 'enlightenment and education' of Jewish workers 'in all subjects bearing on the labour question' and the encouragement of Jewish workers to 'co-operate with English workers in their struggle against the sweating system'.

Jewish Workers and the Unions

It was almost certainly the Manchester IWEC which inspired the first strike of Manchester's Jewish workers. This began in February 1889, at Muratti and Company's cigarette factory on Oxford Road, where a handful of cigarette makers sought to oppose a reduction in piecework rates. Wishing to form a union, but 'largely unacquainted with the methods of working such organisations', a deputation of Jewish workers approached G.D. Kelley,

Morris Zeitlin, a leader of the Manchester branch of the Amalgamated Union of Jewish Tailors and Pressers, with other members of the union. (Courtesy Manchester Jewish Museum.)

secretary of the Manchester and Salford Trades Council, the coordinating body of the local Trade Union movement, for advice. The result was the formation of the Manchester branch of the Cigarette Workers and Tobacco Cutters Union, with Ben Kaplan as its secretary and the majority of its members Jewish. According to Kelley, it was the 21 Jewish workers, out of a total workforce of 28, who spearheaded a strike of which the outcome is not known.

The support of non-Jewish trade unionists was even more evident in the unionization of Jewish workers in the tailoring trade. It was John Marshall, a Manchester organiser of the Amalgamated Society of Tailors (AST), a member of both the Manchester and Salford Trades Council and the Manchester branch of the Socialist League, who in November 1889 convened a meeting in Strangeways to consider ways in which Jewish tailors might best unite with the AST, in improving working conditions in the trade as a whole. The result, in the

Strike meeting of Jewish waterproof garment makers in Derby Hall, Cheetham Hill, 1938. (Courtesy of Manchester Jewish Museum.)

following month, was the organisation of the 400 Jewish workers in the tailoring trade into the Manchester Jewish Machinists', Tailors' and Pressers' Trade Union, with a Jewish president, Barnett Levine. In April 1890, the union brought 1,500 male and female Jewish workers out on strike for a shorter working day (8am to 8pm), recognized breaks for lunch and tea and an increase in piecework rates. The strike was conducted

The Waterproofer, 1936.

Rae Finkel, a leader of the Manchester waterproof garment workers union, who was awarded the TUC's gold medal for her union work. Here she shows her medal to Bob (later Lord) Thomas. (Courtesy Manchester Jewish Museum.)

according to English Trade Union traditions, with open-air meetings and a march through the city streets, headed by a brass band and a huge banner inscribed 'Jews Union'. It was also a partial success. The masters gave way on hours, but the claim for an increase in piecework rates was reduced by half.

The tailors' strike was followed by a chain reaction of militant action by Jewish workers in the footwear, cloth cap, cabinet-making and waterproof garment-making industries. In the 'rough and cheap classes' of the furniture industry, 140 Jewish workers in the cabinet-making workshops of Ancoats were organised by the beginning of 1890, as the East Manchester branch of the Alliance Association of Cabinet and Chair Makers. Of a committee of seven, which met the cabinet-making masters in May 1890 to argue for improved rates of pay and working conditions, two were Jewish, including the vice-chairman Edward Marcus. The strike which followed involved 'the whole of the men engaged in the cheaper class of cabinet making', including all its Jewish workers. Buoyed up by the support of the Trades Council and non-Jewish workers, the strike was brought to a successful conclusion in June 1890, when the employers accepted the rates of pay demanded by the union.

In the waterproof garment industry, an industry all but created by Jewish entrepreneurs, a majority of the male workforce was Jewish. A Waterproof Garment Makers' Union which was in existence by July 1889 was thus essentially a Jewish union: the union's secretary and its delegate to the Trades Council was the Jewish immigrant, Isidore Sugar. In August 1890, with the encouragement of the Trades Council, the union formulated a series of demands which included a maximum working week of 59 hours, a limited advance on piecework rates and the ending of a system of so-called apprenticeships, which had effectively enabled the masters to employ new workers on starvation wages. When these demands were refused, a strike was called which began with a march of 500 waterproofers and 850 tailors to Belle Vue for a meeting under the chairmanship of G.D. Kelley. The strike ended early in September, when the employers accepted the workers' demands with only minor amendments.

In 1890 the 'cheaper end' of boot and shoe-making trades was also dominated by Jewish workers, who formed over half the 600 members of the Manchester branch of the National Union of Boot and Shoe Operatives. A strike in 1890, timed to coincide with a time of maximum consumer demand and following the success of the waterproofers, aimed chiefly at a 'levelling-up' of the pay of Jewish

A Bulletin of the Manchester branch of Waterproof Garment Workers Trade Union (WGWTU), of which most of the members were Jewish, issued during a strike in 1934.

workers to create uniform rates of pay throughout the industry. After picking off individual employers, the union won the acceptance of a new log which gave the lowest paid workers increases from 10 per cent to 20 per cent.

During 1889–91, Jewish immigrant workers in Manchester, following those in Leeds and London, emerged not as the docile victims or apologists of sweating, but as its most militant opponents. The *Manchester Guardian* commented: 'Today the Jew is as ardent a trade unionist as any Englishman, and often far more voluble'. This was also an effective counter to anti-alien propaganda. One Jewish worker commented in 1890: 'We live in a free country…then let us strive to be free men. Don't give our English brothers the chance to point the finger of scorn at us, and say that we work for less wages than them.' To the Jewish middle classes, unionisation was welcome proof of the workers' 'power to assimilate with their surroundings and with

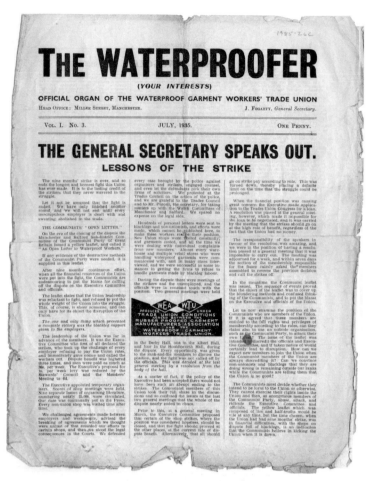

Issue of The Waterproofer, *the official newsletter of the WGWTU, 1935.*

the manners and customs of the land of their adoption'.

The successful strikes of 1889–90, and the creation of new unions of Jewish workers, laid the basis for what became a continuous battle between Jewish workers and Jewish bosses for better conditions in the immigrant trades. It was not an easy battle. Given the existence of a large (and growing) immigrant workforce, Jewish employers were able to renege on their undertakings and then to counter complaints by hiring 'greeners' arriving at Victoria Station. Potential unemployment during the 'slack' seasons in the clothing trades, gave the employers a further bargaining chip. For Jewish workers, there were always the seductive attractions of 'masterdom'. Gains were difficult to make and easy to lose; Jewish workers were easily intimidated. Any backsliding by Jewish workers, moreover, was an injury not only to themselves, but to their non-Jewish fellow-workers, who had helped them in pursuit of their own improvement, and who occasionally expressed their irritation by throwing in their lot with the anti-aliens.

Jews and the Left

A tradition of militant trade unionism and left-wing politics within the Manchester Jewish workforce persisted until the collapse of the immigrant industries in the years which followed World War Two. People of Jewish origin, women as well as men, were involved in each stage of the development of Socialism, Communism and Trade Unionism in Manchester between the 1890s and the 1930s.

Chapter 5

Religious Diversity, 1881–1914

In 1881, there were still only four major synagogues in Manchester: the Great, the Reform, the South Manchester and the Spanish and Portuguese. None of the immigrant chevroth, perhaps 20 in all by 1881, had as yet emerged from the domestic premises in which they had taken root in Red Bank and Strangeways. A central theme in the religious history of the community, between the 1880s and World War One, consists of the imprint made on the community by immigrant religious aspirations: the conversion of some of the larger chevroth into major synagogues, and the creation of institutions which embodied the distinctive religious aspirations, needs and standards of the immigrant poor.

Hazan Newman and the Great Synagogue Choir, c.1920. (Courtesy Manchester Jewish Museum.)

Chevroth and Synagogues

Typically, as the membership of a miniscule chevra increased in number and as some of its originally working-class members became workshop masters, warehousemen or major shopkeepers, the impulse of its leaders was to convert it into a place of worship which would reflect its size and the improving status of its membership. Again typically, the chevra would then seek out more salubrious premises, raise sufficient funds to appoint a qualified rabbi, preferably a scholar of Eastern European origin, and seek legitimacy, including the right to register marriages, by placing themselves under the authority of the Chief Rabbi in London, recognised since the early 19th century as the spiritual guide of British Jewry. The conversion of domestic chevroth into synagogues was, in this way, the religious reflection of the improving economic status and increasing social integration of sectors of the immigrant

Religious and lay dignitaries of the Manchester Jewish Community in the Succah of the Great Synagogue, 1923. (Courtesy Manchester Jewish Museum.)

*The New Synagogue,
Cheetham Hill Road,
1889. (Courtesy Jewish
Heritage UK and the
Glyn Family.)*

*Interior of the New
Synagogue, 1889.
(Courtesy Jewish
Heritage UK and the
Glyn family.)*

*The Holy Law Beth
Aaron Synagogue,
otherwise 'Claff's Shule,'
on Bank View above Red
Bank, 1891. (Courtesy
Jewish Heritage UK and
the Glyn family.)*

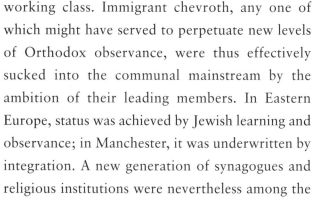

working class. Immigrant chevroth, any one of which might have served to perpetuate new levels of Orthodox observance, were thus effectively sucked into the communal mainstream by the ambition of their leading members. In Eastern Europe, status was achieved by Jewish learning and observance; in Manchester, it was underwritten by integration. A new generation of synagogues and religious institutions were nevertheless among the earliest symptoms of the growing communal influence of the immigrant nouveau riches.

The first of these newly emerging places of worship was the Manchester New Synagogue and Beth Hamedrash (House of Study) whose founders, in October 1888, purchased a site on Cheetham Hill Road on which, in 1889, they opened a synagogue built in Romanesque style, with a seating capacity of 400 and a Beth Hamedrash which could accommodate 200 readers. Its founders, each of whom paid between £10 and £25 towards the building costs, were chiefly shopkeepers, travellers and workshop masters of Russo-Polish origin, drawn from a variety of the chevroth and whose (forlorn) hope was to bring the congregants of all the chevroth together under one roof. In 1893 the synagogue appointed Isaac Jacob Reiness of Lida, a distinguished Russian Rabbi and scholar, as its first minister, his arrival in Manchester greeted by 'dense crowds' which lined the route from Victoria Station into Cheetham Hill Road.

The brash Eastern European nouveau riches who founded the New Synagogue possessed a far more assertive Jewish identity than the elite members of the Great Synagogue, the so-called 'Englischer Schule'

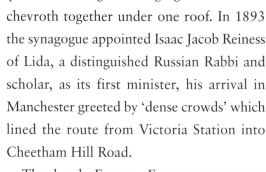

(English Synagogue), who chose to play down their Jewishness in public, to remain silent in the face of anti-Semitism and to place stress on their acculturation. One story of their relationship dates from a local scandal about the so-called excesses of moneylenders in 1890s

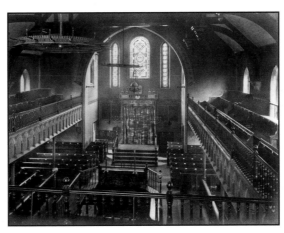

Interior of the Holy Law Beth Aaron Synagogue. (Courtesy Jewish Heritage UK and Glyn family.)

Manchester. The defensive response of the Great Synagogue was to ban 'financiers' from membership of the synagogue. On hearing this, it is said, the committee of the New Synagogue introduced a new congregational law which stated there must be at least one moneylender on every committee of the synagogue. This assertiveness was to express itself in more significant ways such as the support Eastern European alrightniks provided to the religious aspirations of the immigrant poor, and in their backing of the infant Zionist movement.

On 1 November 1891 another group of immigrant businessmen, 'nearly all…from the town of Brody' (in Austrian Galicia), met in Irwell Street, Strangeways, to plan a synagogue which would bring together their Galician co-religionists in forms of worship familiar to them in their homeland. This 'Brodyer Synagogue', opening on 6 December 1891 in a rented house in Strangeways, moved in June 1893 into a converted Greek church and mission house on Waterloo Road and finally, in 1899, into the converted premises of a Methodist New Connexion place of worship (Salem Chapel) on Bury New Road where, because it had then opened its doors to immigrants from other parts of Eastern Europe, its name was changed to the North Manchester Synagogue. By the end of 1900 it had 175 members including, according to contemporary reports, some from the Strangeways chevroth which it had absorbed.

In 1870 the Chevra Walkawishk, created in Red Bank during the 1860s by immigrants from a town of that name in western Russia, had appointed the fiery Russian scholar and orator, Susman Cohen, as its Rabbi. Cohen was a man of uncompromising Orthodox observance held in awe by the immigrant poor and viewed with some anxiety by the anglicised middle classes of the Great

Samuel Claff's wife, Bertha, in fancy dress.

Samuel Claff, a furniture dealer and moneylender of Russian origin, a prominent Zionist, founder of the Holy Law Beth Aaron Synagogue and one of the founders of the Manchester Jewish Hospital. (Courtesy Manchester Jewish Museum.)

Interior of the United Synagogue. (Courtesy Manchester Jewish Museum.)

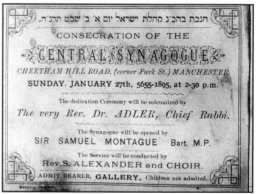

Invitation to the opening of the Central Synagogue, 1894.

The Central Synagogue at the corner of Park Street and Cheetham Hill Road, 1894. (Courtesy Jewish Heritage UK and the Glyn family.)

Synagogue. Moving in 1889 into larger premises, the chevra became the Fernie Street New Synagogue. Then, seeking premises large enough to include a school room, a library and reading room, the congregation purchased a former Wesleyan Chapel at the corner of Park Street and Cheetham Hill Road, where it opened as the Central Synagogue in the autumn of 1894. Following a long and fierce dispute with the Great Synagogue over an independent *shechita* by which it had sought to raise funds, it finally acknowledged the authority of the Chief Rabbi to become 'a properly constituted synagogue'. In December 1894 Susman Cohen left Manchester to become a judge on the Chief Rabbi's *Beth Din* (Ecclesiastical Court) in London, leaving behind what was generally seen as Manchester's most traditionally Orthodox congregation.

In September 1891 the Chevra Torah (the Society of the Holy Law), perhaps the oldest of the Red Bank chevroth, said to have been created by placing

corrugated iron over two backyards, moved to larger premises (formerly a church) above Red Bank on Bank View, which were purchased and converted by the Russian immigrant moneylender, Samuel Aaron Claff. There, with seating accommodation for 200 men and 150 women, it reinvented itself as the Holy Law Synagogue. Known locally as 'Claff's *Shool*' or 'Beth Aaron' (the House of Aaron), in the following year it received official recognition by the Chief Rabbi and, two years later, brought over its own rabbi from Russia to work under the Chief Rabbi's supervision.

The New, North Manchester, Central, and Holy Law synagogues were the most important of the new synagogues which had their roots in Eastern European chevroth. The further history of religious change between the 1880s and 1920 has the quality of a kaleidoscope shaken at intervals throughout the period of mass immigration. Each new batch of immigrants (so-called 'greeners') created new chevroth as their first cultural and social bases in Manchester. In time these disappeared,

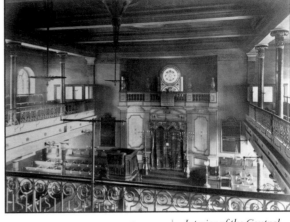

Interior of the Central Synagogue. (Courtesy Jewish Heritage UK and the Glyn family.)

amalgamated (with each other or with an existing synagogue) or emerged as 'properly constituted synagogues' to be replaced, in their turn, by still more chevroth as the influx from Russia and Romania continued, unabated, until checked by the outbreak of war. Some premises, most notably 78 Cheetham Hill Road, the former premises of the Jews' School, and 59 Cheetham Hill Road, a loft above a shop, selling hay for horses (hence the 'Hayshop Schule'), became places of transit for a number of former chevroth passing through, so to speak, on their way to becoming synagogues. In any one year between 1890 and 1914, the religious make-up of the community reflects all these cyclical processes. Among other new synagogues to emerge were the Lower Broughton in Cambridge Street (1891), the Strangeways Synagogue in Harris Street (1893) and the Romanian Synagogue in Briddon Street, Strangeways (1899). Another Romanian Synagogue, which adopted the Sephardi ritual, was opened on Waterloo Road by Haham Moses Gaster on 4 September 1904.

Rabbi Israel Yoffey, rabbi of the Central Synagogue, 1898. (Courtesy Manchester Jewish Museum.)

Most chevroth were at first determined to maintain their strict standards of religious observance throughout their upward progress to synagogue status. Although certainly seeking prestige within the orbit of the Chief Rabbinate, their hope was that they would not lose their links with Eastern European traditions for religious scholarship, strict orthodox observance, short services and long Talmudic discourses from ministers of the stamp of Susman Cohen. In reality, most moved irreversibly in the direction of compromise. Links with Eastern Europe were broken. Religious scholarship lost its hold on a new generation. Services lengthened, Talmudic discourses were replaced by the rhetoric of English moralism and religious observance flagged. The first to maintain, with any success, the traditions of Eastern Europe was the Kehal

The North Manchester Synagogue, formerly the Brodyer Shule, on Cheetham Hill Road, 1899. (Courtesy Jewish Heritage UK and the Glyn family.)

Chassidim (now Adath Israel), founded in 1896 as the last incumbent of the 'Hayshop Schule' of 59 Cheetham Hill Road and the first expression, in Manchester, of Eastern European *Chassidism*. Otherwise the emergence of Eastern European synagogues served as a kind of religious stimulant which maintained, and often strengthened, the standards of Orthodox observance throughout the community.

Minor Synagogues

A synagogue of a unique kind was the small 'Bent Street Free Synagogue' set up in the late 1880s by Haim Besso, a Sephardi merchant from Corfu, after he had fallen out with the committee of the Spanish and Portuguese Synagogue on congregational ritual and government matters. Situated in Bent Street, backing onto Cheetham Hill Road almost opposite the Spanish and Portuguese, and better known in the community as 'Mr Besso's Synagogue', it survived until January 1932 largely, it is said, through the support of Besso's relatives and

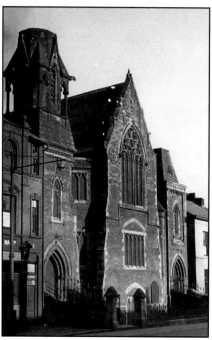

The Manchester United Synagogue, founded in 1904 in a former Methodist Chapel by a breakaway group who supported a rabbi controversially dismissed from the New Synagogue. (Courtesy Manchester Central Library.)

friends. Its form of democracy was best expressed in an invitation card sent to prospective members: 'Every member of this synagogue will be a vice-president.' On its closure, the synagogue furniture was transferred to the *Talmud Torah*, also in Bent Street (see below), to comprise the Talmud Torah's own synagogue.

Finally, tiny synagogues emerged on the borders of Christian working-class communities in Manchester and Salford which had attracted Jewish pawnbrokers, and Jewish retailers of jewellery and clothing, seeking a market outside the competitive Jewish Quarter and the expensive city centre. By the early 1890s at least six such 'shopkeeper colonies' had emerged, each with sufficient males to make up a minyan for public worship. Typically, a room above one of the shops would be used for public service, sufficiently often for it to be described within the community and in the Jewish press as a synagogue. So, a Miles Platting Synagogue was in existence by 1894, a Rochdale Road Synagogue and a Pendleton Synagogue by 1896, along with more temporary minyanim in Hulme, on Ashton Old Road and in Butler Street, Ancoats; all districts well beyond the Jewish Quarter and without substantial settlements of Jewish families. On Oxford Road, Chorlton-on-Medlock, local Jewish shopkeepers created two places of worship between 1890 and 1914 which coexisted into the 1930s: the Oxford Road Hebrew Congregation and the New Oxford Road Synagogue, although records do not exist to explain their differences. Other small bodies of adventurous Jewish shopkeepers created synagogues in such nearby towns as Stockport (1891), Oldham and Blackburn (1893).

Samuel Small (formerly Smolensky) with his children outside his second-hand clothing shop in Jackson's Avenue, Hulme. It was typical of the small shops set up by Jewish retailers on the edge of large residential areas of the English working class. (Courtesy Manchester Jewish Museum.)

The Manchester Talmud Torah

It was the Eastern Europeans who, with their greater religious zeal and stricter observance of Jewish custom, created institutions designed to educate a younger generation in matters of religion and to ensure the observance of Jewish religious law. In 1879 Mrs Rose Fineberg, a Manchester housewife from Kalverie, a township in Russian Poland, is said to have conceived the idea of making provision for the education in Hebrew and religion of the children of the Jewish poor. According to this account, 'she picked up half a dozen boys and placed them in charge of a Hebrew teacher whom she persuaded to give his services gratis'. She then convened a meeting at the house of a friend, Mrs Joseph Taylor, where funds were collected for renting a small room in Winter Street, Red Bank, as a makeshift Talmud Torah (religious

Louis Fidler, a Lithuanian Jewish immigrant, outside his ironmonger's shop in Regent Road, Salford, on the borders of another working-class residential district. The Jewish shopkeepers on Regent Road established their own minyan for Sabbath Services held above one of their shops. (Courtesy Manchester Jewish Museum.)

school) for those immigrant children whose parents could not afford to find them a private tutor. After several moves to rented premises in the lower part of Cheetham Hill, in 1889 the school moved to a building in Bent Street said to consist of only two large whitewashed rooms with long tables and benches. Finally, on 6 August 1894, the foundation stone was laid of new premises on the same site, which were occupied in the following December, consecrated by the Chief Rabbi in January 1895 and which were rumoured to be, then, the only purpose-built Talmud Torah in the British Empire. Its local non-Jewish architect, the eccentric William Sharp Ogden, had earlier designed the New Synagogue. There is nothing 'Jewish' about the Talmud Torah building apart, perhaps, from a (botched) attempt to represent the Star of David on the exterior brickwork. Those who could afford it paid 1d a week for their lessons; the rest received free tuition. Immigrant children would attend two or three times a week after their day in secular school and on Sunday mornings to be taught by Revd Israel Slotki, appointed as the school's Superintendent in 1911, or by one of his volunteer instructors.

The Manchester Yeshiva

A higher education in religion and Hebrew was not available in Manchester until 1911 when, on the initiative of three immigrant rabbis, a group of Orthodox businessmen created the Manchester Yeshiva (otherwise the Manchester Talmudical College), in 'cramped premises' in Broughton Street, Cheetham. After moving from one rented premises to another, in 1919 it settled into a house at 215 Cheetham Hill Road donated by the Manchester businessman, Baruch Meir Bloom. From the beginning, the *Yeshiva* saw itself as a 'spiritual lighthouse', serving to counteract the assimilatory tendencies which its founders saw as undermining the 'true observance' of the communal young.

Most students were admitted to full or part-time courses at the age of 13 and left at 16 when they were expected to serve as exemplars in the community of Jewish Orthodox learning and observance. Only a few carefully selected students stayed on after 16 to train as rabbis, ministers, shochetim or religious teachers. Under Rabbi Moshe Yitzchak Segal, recruited in 1913 from the London Yeshiva as its Principal, the Yeshiva came to see itself as a centre of religious learning on a par with the long-established seats of Jewish learning in Eastern Europe.

The Manchester Shechita Board and the Beth Din

Most newly emerging synagogues had financed their early progress and asserted their supposedly superior orthodoxy by creating independent structures for

The Manchester Talmud Torah at the time of a visit to Manchester from the Londoner Sir Montagu Samuel in 1894.

shechita: mechanisms which controlled the production and sale of kosher meat. While the very existence of an independent shechita suggested the high religious standards of those who created it, the taxes paid by the appointed butchers helped finance new buildings and the appointment of prestigious rabbis. To the Great Synagogue which had, from its beginnings, controlled shechita for the community as a whole, such actions were perceived as rebellious snubs which also dented income from which, for example, it had subsidised the Jewish Board of Guardians. The transformation of a chevra into a synagogue thus usually involved a communal conflict over the control of shechita, usually ending in the Great Synagogue's favour, although not without a lengthy battle, by the intervention of the Chief Rabbi.

In the longer term, a compromise solution was found in the creation of a communal *Shechita Board*, in 1892, which represented both the older synagogues and the newly emerging Eastern European places of worship. On a Board of Management of 16 members, five were drawn from the Great Synagogue, four from the New, three each from the South Manchester and the Spanish and Portuguese, and two each from the Central and the Holy Law. Of

Barmitzvah photograph of Henry Greenberg. (Courtesy Manchester Jewish Museum.)

The Manchester Talmud Torah, 1898. (Courtesy Jewish Heritage UK and the Glyn family.)

the Board's three ecclesiastical supervisors, who also, at first unofficially, decided on matters of Jewish Law, two were Eastern European immigrant rabbis (at first Susman Cohen and Mendel Dagutsky) and one was the rabbi of the Great Synagogue. The hope was that, in removing the sole supervision of communal shechita from the Great Synagogue and involving of the Eastern European sector of communal life in shechita management, religious peace would reign in the community. This did not immediately turn out to be the case. Instead of emerging synagogues warring with the Great Synagogue for the right to an independent shechita, each now battled in turn with the Shechita Board to the same purpose.

The Shechita Board nevertheless emerged as a major communal institution. Apart from supervising the supply of kosher meat, granting licences to butchers and liaising with the Chief Rabbi on the registration of shochetim, the Board now 'undertook all those communal burdens hitherto carried out by the Great Synagogue'. This included a subsidy of £250 a year to the Jewish Board of Guardians and the supply of matzos to the Jewish poor at the time of Passover. In the absence of any other institution whose jurisdiction ranged over the whole community, the Board also began to see itself as exercising a degree of coordination over communal affairs and as a means of mediation between the Jewish community and wider society. In October 1896 it explicitly accorded itself the right 'to safeguard generally the interests of the community, and take cognizance of all matters which concern its welfare and dignity'. On the religious side, in 1902 the Shechita Board converted its three supervisors into an official Beth Din (ecclesiastical court) to adjudicate on matters related to shechita and to deliver decisions on other matters of Jewish Law, such as the issue of divorces. In this, as in other matters, the pressure of Eastern European immigrants had moved the community towards a greater respect for Jewish religious tradition.

Chapter 6

The Philanthropic Tradition, 1881–1914

According to Walter Tomlinson, writing of Manchester in 1887, 'one of the most noteworthy and interesting features of the social economy of our Jews is the abounding and wise charity exercised toward those of their own nation, come whence they may'. As a voluntary society, with such distinct needs as kosher food and Sabbath observance, and with its own traditions of charity *(Zedaka)*, the Jewish community had little option but to create a parallel structure of social welfare, dependent for its effective working largely on voluntary effort and paid for chiefly by voluntary contributions. Fundraising was thus a constant communal preoccupation, the history of communal philanthropy being littered with appeals and charity events and with calls to members of the community to play their part as subscribers, collectors, canvassers or volunteer workers.

Anglicisation

The evolution and success of Jewish trade unionism was welcome to the established Jewish leadership as evidence of the powers of integration of the immigrant working class, provided only that it did not include any brand of militant socialism which might associate the community with public disorder.

The conversion of the 'immigrant masses' into respectable members of an anglicised community was also a major objective of Jewish education and philanthropy. Once it was recognised that the mass of Jewish immigrants from Eastern Europe, when they had found work and accommodation in Manchester, could not readily be 'moved on' in the direction of Liverpool and the United States, they became the objects of middle-class charity. Part of this was a recognition by the established community that it could not ignore the well-being of immigrant co-religionists. Talmudic teaching demanded that they be the objects of communal charity. Part, however, was a continuation of the anglicising pressures which had been applied since the formation of the Jews' School and

Miss Hannah Raphael, the formidable headmistress of the girls' section of the Manchester Jews' School from 1887 to 1923. (Courtesy Manchester Jewish Museum.)

Cheetham Assembly Rooms, Cheetham Hill Road, a favoured venue for Jewish social and fund-raising events. (Copyright Manchester Central Library.)

Class at the Manchester Jews' School, 1921. (Courtesy Manchester Jewish Museum.)

the Jewish Board of Guardians. Material support was given only to those considered deserving and then only to those prepared to exchange membership of chevroth for seat-holding in a respectable English synagogue, and to submit their children to the anglicising influences of the Jews' School. As the proportion of new immigrants in the community expanded rapidly from the 1880s, the intensity of anglicisation consequently increased.

The Jewish Ladies Visiting Association

In May 1884, a small number of women from the richer and longer-established Manchester Jewish families created what was to become a major communal charity, the Jewish Ladies Visiting Association. Like the Jewish Board of Guardians and most other communal charities, the JLVA was modelled on a voluntary organisation in the wider society – the Manchester and Salford Ladies Sanitary Association – which, in one form or another, had been active in the city since the early 1850s. The aim of the Ladies Sanitary Association, made up chiefly of middle-class Christian women, was 'to promote attention to personal and domestic cleanliness, to temperance and to the laws of heath generally, and to induce co-operation with the authorities in giving effect to official regulations for sanitary improvement'. This was to be achieved by visits to homes in districts believed to require 'sanitary improvement', by the mounting of lectures on public health and by the distribution to the poor of tracts written 'in plain language'. The city was divided into districts, each with a voluntary 'lady superintendent', drawn from the society's middle-class membership, aided by a paid 'mission woman', whose task it was to organise and manage such 'civilising' activities as sewing classes, mothers' meetings, savings banks, clothing clubs, readings from the classics and Bible lessons, and to provide poor families, when required, with nourishing meals, nursing, cheap lodgings, medicines, washing powder and carbolic soap. A scheme was devised to provide cheap (or free) holidays for the children of the poor. The underlying assumptions behind the work of visiting were that the poor would learn from the example of the rich and that an 'association of the classes' would also limit the possibility of public disorder.

In 1882, when the Ladies Sanitary Association first decided to bring 'the truly populous [and Jewish] part of Strangeways' within its scope, it attracted the interest of a number of well-to-do Jewish women including Anna Simmons, wife of the minister of the Reform Synagogue, Lawrence Mark Simmons; Abigail Behrens, the daughter of Philip Lucas and wife of the wealthy cotton merchant and manufacturer Edward Behrens; and Hedwig Dreyfus, wife of the industrial chemist Dr Charles Dreyfus, who had arrived from Alsace-Lorraine in the late 1860s and who, in 1870, had set up a factory manufacturing dyes in the Clayton district of Manchester. All were members of the Reform Synagogue, the Jewish place of worship with the closest links to the city elite. Abigail Behrens, in particular, was already involved in civic philanthropy. As a member of the Manchester Association for Promoting the Education of Women, she had been active in the establishment of the Manchester High School for Girls, the first Manchester institution to take the academic education

Teachers at the Manchester Jews' School, 1910. (Courtesy Manchester Jewish Museum.)

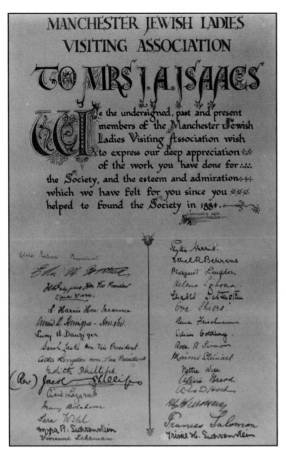

*Illuminated address
presented to Isaac Asher
Isaacs, secretary of the
Jewish Board of
Guardians, by the
Jewish Ladies Visiting
Association.*

of middle-class women seriously, in its own words: 'to provide for Manchester's daughters what had been provided with out stint [by Manchester Grammar School] for Manchester's sons'. She was also involved in the Ancoats Recreation Movement, which from the late 1870s had sought to bring high art, fine music and informed debate to the working classes of Ancoats.

The JLVA was founded at a meeting of women at the Behrens mansion, the Oaks, in Fallowfield on 6 May 1884. All were young; all of English or German birth, all women of leisure whose homes and children were managed by servants; in the case of Abigail Behrens, by an army of 19. Abigail Behrens was elected to the chair, with Hedwig Dreyfus as treasurer and Anna Simmons as joint secretary with Amy Straus, the wife of a textile exporter living in Bowdon. The Association was a Jewish replica of the Ladies Sanitary Association, its formation a classic example of Christian institutions being adapted for Jewish purposes. The overall aim was 'to inculcate a high standard of hygiene among the people visited, and to teach, wherever possible, such habits as may help to prevent the beginnings of disease'. It was also, like the Sanitary Association, a civilising mechanism. Each lady visitor undertook to visit at least five houses, once a fortnight, to monitor their sanitary condition, to 'give such advice as would promote thrift and domestic and personal cleanliness, and to encourage habits of self-supporting industry'. They were required also, 'if it can be conveniently and discreetly managed, to see the rent books each time they visit'. Among the items distributed by the visitors were material for making clothes (most of it from their husbands' warehouses), disinfecting powder and carbolic soap, which was ordered by the hundredweight.

Drawing on the experience of the Sanitary Association, the JLVA developed rapidly into a major communal institution. In September 1884, when the constituency of the JLVA was widened to include Red Bank and a group of impoverished Jewish families living around Crown Square in Angel Meadow, Mrs Annie Levy of Glasgow was appointed as a paid district visitor, the equivalent of the Sanitary Association's mission women. A second district visitor was added in 1891. Part of their job was to liaise with the sympathetic health authorities of the city, with power to call on the Manchester medical officer of health, to apply pressure on landlords who refused to keep their properties in good condition.

The Home for Aged, Sick and Incurable Jews, c.1900. (Courtesy Jewish Heritage UK and the Glyn family.)

One by one, more specialist services were added to the Association's work. By the end of 1889 these included regular mothers' meetings, a sick and nourishment department which distributed tickets for free milk and meat to the 'deserving sick', a works branch which offered token payments to unemployed women for making up materials into finished garments, Monday evening social gatherings at which the poor were taught English, arithmetic and needlework (and rubbed shoulders with the rich), a savings bank, and a rescue and protection service to deal with Jewish women said to be 'living a life of ill-fame'. In 1891 Anna Simmons began collecting funds to establish summer holidays for the children of the poor, first at a cottage near New Mills and, from 1895, at a holiday home acquired by the Association at Chinley, near Chapel-en-le-Frith. In 1895 200 children were given free holidays at Chinley, 80 at 5s a head. Thus, it was believed, children from 'slum houses' would 'learn something of the beauty of the countryside'. In 1893 the Association mounted its first Sabbath services for working girls at which the women were expected to join the minister in prayer, 'accompanying him in an undertone'.

Synagogue at the Home for the Aged, c.1920. (Courtesy Manchester Jewish Museum.)

Looking back on their work, members of the JLVA saw themselves as having been 'an association of women of leisure, desirous of helping their less fortunate sisters to conditions of life in which health should not be undermined, energy wasted, and all reasonable happiness and pleasure made impossible, by the terrible conditions imposed on many dwellers in mean streets'. According to one of its founders it also embodied the feminine point of view: 'when work of any kind is to be done, the man so often sees the forest without thinking of the trees, the case of the trees is the woman's part'. In

Rest room at the Home for the Aged, c.1920. (Courtesy Manchester Jewish Museum.)

Jewish Home for the Aged, following periodic extensions, 1940. (Courtesy Manchester Central Library.)

this sense, it was the female arm of the Jewish Board of Guardians with which, from the beginning, it worked in harmony. While the Board, dominated by men, concentrated on financial relief, the JLVA provided more personal services. It also offered one of the few means by which the women of the well-to-do might find a way of playing a role in the life of the community. These same women played key roles in other communal charities. From 1887 the Manchester and Liverpool Jewish Visitation Society delegated the task of visiting the women on their lists to the JLVA as they themselves, since 1884, had organised visits by Jewish ministers of religions to Jewish patients in local hospitals and asylums, Jewish inmates in local workhouses and Jewish prisoners in local gaols. Members of the JLVA supplied successive presidents to the United Sisters Charitable and Benevolent Society, created in the 1840s 'to relieve poor Jewish females (legally married) during their confinement in childbed and sickness'.

The Hebrew Bread, Meat and Coal Society

The Lord Mayor and his party outside the Home for the Aged, c.1919–20. (Courtesy Manchester Jewish Museum.)

In or about 1886, male members of the community created a charity of a unique kind. Known as the Bread, Meat and Coal Society, each of its subscribers received coupons to the value of his subscription which he could then distribute to those he believed to be in need and which could be exchanged in local shops for beef, coal and bread. Subscribers, it was said, thus 'had the satisfaction of relieving those whom they personally knew to be deserving'. Its only overheads were the rent of a small office, paid for by the proceeds of a ball held annually on the festival of Purim. The society appears to have been founded by the local furniture dealer Samson Levi, its other committee members linked to him solely by their membership of Zion Lodge, a Jewish Freemason lodge founded in 1879. In 1895 the presidency of the society passed to Aubrey Franks, who was the eldest son of the founder and first Master of Zion Lodge and grandson of the optician Jacob Franks, a founder member of Manchester Jewry. Another early member of the Bread, Meat and Coal Society was Frederick Hyman who, in 1887, founded and edited the only Jewish newspaper published (although only for a few months) in 19th-century Manchester.

Board room of the Jewish Home for the Aged, c.1920. (Courtesy Manchester Jewish Museum.)

The Bread, Meat and Coal Society was also the communal charity which provided the first foothold in communal administration to manufacturers and merchants of Eastern European origin who, in the 1880s, were beginning to challenge the monopoly of communal power exercised by textile merchants of German, Dutch and Sephardi origin. One was Mark Doniger, a Russian immigrant and partner in what was fast becoming the largest Manchester factory for the manufacture of cloth caps. The secretaryship of the society was also the first communal office of Nathan Laski who, after World War One, was to emerge as the lay leader of the community. Born in Brisk in the Polish-speaking region of Russia, Laski arrived in England in the late 1860s with his father, a travelling jeweller. After settling first in Leeds, then in Middlesbrough, the family moved on in the mid-1870s to Manchester, where Nathan became a pupil at the Manchester Jews' School. After leaving school he found a place as a clerk in the offices of the Manchester textile exporters, Gunnis and Company. In 1886, when he joined the committee of the Bread, Meat and Coal Society, he had become the firm's manager and also a prominent member of the Liberal Party in Cheetham Hill. In the same year he was initiated into Zion Lodge.

Out-patients department at the Manchester Jewish Hospital. (Courtesy Manchester Jewish Museum.)

The Jewish Soup Kitchen

It was men and women from among these immigrant nouveaux riches, including Michael Marks of Marks and Spencer, now living in handsome new property in Higher Broughton, who in February

Waiting room at the Jewish Hospital. (Courtesy Manchester Jewish Museum.)

1895 joined with the minister of the Great Synagogue, Rabbi Dr Berendt Salomon, to open a temporary soup kitchen for the Jewish residents of Red Bank. Judging the experiment to have been a success, on 1 January 1896 a permanent Manchester Soup Kitchen for the Jewish Poor was established in rented rooms in Lord Street where, three times a week, those judged to be in need were given 'a can of soup and two loaves'. After considering other sites for a larger building to meet a growing demand, in June 1906 the kitchen moved into purpose-built premises in Southall Street, where it was named 'Philanthropic Hall', and was officially opened by the Lord Mayor of Manchester and the waterproof garment manufacturer Isidore Frankenburg, then Mayor of Salford. Like the managers of the Jewish Hospital, the organisers of the Soup Kitchen prided themselves on opening its services to non-Jews working in the Cheetham area.

The Home for Aged, Sick and Incurable Jews

Another major philanthropic institution was the Home for Aged, Sick and Incurable Jews and Temporary Shelter. In its beginnings, it was an offshoot of the Bread, Meat and Coal Society. In March 1888 the society's chairman, Samson Levi, set aside a surplus of £50 to open a fund for the provision of a home for the Jewish elderly 'on the same principles as the London home'. By October 1892 the fund had risen to £500, still far less than was required to acquire and equip the necessary premises. It was not until January 1898, after the cap-making entrepreneur Jacob Doniger had offered a house rent free at 28 Elizabeth Street, that Aubrey Franks, then chairman of the Bread, Meat and Coal Society, was able to announce the imminent opening of 'a comfortable house to maintain and clothe those aged, respectable and indigent persons of the Jewish religion' aged over the age of 60 and who had lived in Manchester at least five years. With space at first for only eight residents, the home expanded when Doniger offered larger premises in 1902. There was

Operating Theatre, Manchester Jewish Hospital. (Courtesy Manchester Jewish Museum.)

space for 20 beds at 208 Cheetham Hill Road, the site which the home was to occupy for the next half century. When the home was full to capacity, other Jewish elderly people were found lodgings in the community at the expense of the home, to which they came for their meals. In November 1906, the home amalgamated with a temporary shelter set up some years earlier by the wine merchant A.J. Epstein, 'to assist those of his poor co-religionists who might find themselves stranded without friends or means in their migratory search for the means of subsistence'.

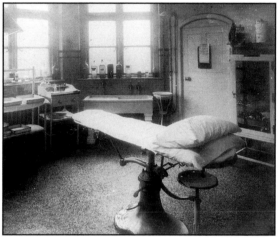

The Jewish Hospital

The initiative for the creation of the JLVA, the Home for the Aged, the Soup Kitchen and the Bread, Meat and Coal Society had come from the Jewish middle classes. Once set in train, they developed without conflict in terms of middle-class perceptions of the needs of the poor, the elderly or the infirm. This was not the case with what became, in 1904, the Manchester Victoria Memorial Jewish Hospital.

Ward at the Manchester Jewish Hospital. (Courtesy Manchester Jewish Museum.)

The initiative in this case came from working-class immigrants' expression of their own needs: the movement for a Jewish hospital, according to one of its promoters, had 'sprung up spontaneously among the poor themselves'. The response of the middle classes was divided: some were willing to satisfy immigrant needs, while others were inclined to see them as dangerous to the security of the community. The conflict that resulted was also personal, as a

Group of the founders of the Manchester Jewish Hospital, 1904. (Courtesy Manchester Jewish Hospital.)

struggle for supremacy between two leading figures in the community emerged. Dr Charles Dreyfus, the chemical engineer, Conservative city councillor and Zionist, championed immigrant aspirations, while Nathan Laski believed the plan for a Jewish Hospital (as for a Zionist future) would suggest the community's insularity. Laski's preference was for Jewish involvement in British politics and for an adaptation of local hospitals to serve Jewish needs.

After several false starts, the movement for the creation of a Jewish hospital took off in the summer of 1900 when the immigrant poor's aspirations for a hospital close at hand, which met their particular religious needs and where they might be treated alongside other Yiddish-speakers, were taken up by a group of workshop masters, merchants and professional men (including two GPs), all of Eastern European origin. Prominent among them was the Russian moneylender Samuel Claff, who became chairman of the Land and Buildings Committee, and the Romanian physician, Dr Joseph Dulberg. The hospital, they believed, was necessary to the health of immigrants reluctant to risk the cultural discomfort of treatment in any city hospital. Even 'in their last fight with death they wished to have their own friends around them'. It may be that the promoters also saw a Jewish hospital as an adequate response to the Christian missionary clinics which were emerging within the Jewish Quarter, in which treatment was combined with an effort to convert. As soon as the proposition became a subject for public debate, it attracted the opposition of a body of the Jewish well-to-do, led by Nathan Laski, for whom it challenged the shared notion of Jewish 'integration'. Laski spoke scathingly of 'the Jewish Hospital Ghetto'. He and his allies also doubted the ability of the 'hospital group' to support the new institution, as they had prophesied, from the 'pennies of the poor' rather than the donations of the rich. For Laski, there were better options: a 'kosher kitchen' to supply all Manchester hospitals or perhaps a 'Jewish ward' in the Manchester Royal Infirmary (MRI), then considering a move to a new site.

The 'hospital party' was immensely strengthened when, in mid-September 1900, Dr Charles Dreyfus accepted an invitation to chair it. His motives are uncertain. It may be that, as a leading Zionist, he saw himself as a protector of immigrant aspirations. It also seems likely that the hospital project offered him a power base from which he might challenge the growing authority of Nathan Laski, who had cemented his communal prestige by his election as the youngest-ever president of the Great Synagogue. It may be that there was an element of political rivalry, for while Dreyfus was a Conservative city councillor, Laski was a leading Liberal whose wife, Sarah, was a Liberal city councillor.

Illuminated address presented to Nathan Laski for his services to the Jewish Hospital. (Courtesy Manchester Jewish Museum.)

Whatever the case, Laski and Dreyfus became leaders of the two 'camps' into which the *Jewish Chronicle* saw the community divided on the hospital issue. After several public debates, some of them tempestuous, what finally undermined the opposition was the decision of the MRI to rebuild in south Manchester, well away from the Jewish Quarter. By the summer of 1903, even Laski had given up with the scheme. Land had been purchased in Elizabeth Street, Cheetham, and architect's plans had been agreed for the construction of a small hospital. On 17 November 1904 a two-storey building with four wards, eight beds, an operating theatre and an accident department was officially opened as the Manchester Victoria Memorial Jewish Hospital; the name emerging as a result of those who had accused the hospital's supporters of being 'insular', 'exclusive' or 'particularist'. From the beginning, as in the case of the Soup Kitchen, the hospital took pride in the fact that it was open to non-Jews living in the district; by 1908 the number of beds had increased to 40.

It is indicative of Nathan Laski's political skill that within very few years he had become the hospital's president, a further step on a ladder that was to lead, by the late 1920s, to an unchallenged leadership of the community which lasted until his death in a motor accident in 1941.

Chapter 7

Immigrant Self-Help, 1875–1914

The Jewish Hospital might be seen as an example of immigrant self-help. Although in time it attracted large donations from the well-to-do, its immediate future was based squarely, as its promoters had promised, on weekly collections of 'pennies from the poor'. The results of such collections were duly recorded in the hospital's reports. To be a collector was a matter of pride, expressed in a succession of collectors' clubs, each with its own programme of social events.

Jewish Friendly Societies

Equally spectacular, as an indication that immigrants from Eastern Europe were not prepared to depend on the often condescending and typically assimilationist charity of the Jewish rich, was the proliferation in Manchester

Executives of the Manchester Branch of the Jewish Workers Circle Friendly Society, 1909. Morris Zeitlin is fourth from the left, back row. (Courtesy Manchester Jewish Museum.)

during the 1890s of Jewish Friendly Societies. Based on the societies which had been multiplying in wider society since the 1820s, the Jewish Friendly Societies were the means by which poorer workers might insure themselves against the cost of sickness, death and unemployment during the seven days of mourning *(shiva)* which followed the death of a parent. In some cases there was also a sharing of a society's surplus funds at Passover. Some Friendly Societies began as (and remained) independent creations of groups of Jewish workers. In time, most belonged to one or another of the Orders which, like their equivalent in Christian society, evolved to give administrative discipline, stability, procedural uniformity and public prestige to their 'branches'. Most Jewish Orders had Jewish names: one, whose derivation from an English model was more explicit, called itself the Grand Order of Hebrew Druids.

Immensely popular within the more aspiring sectors of working-class Jewry, the total membership (all male) of Friendly Societies probably exceeded that of the Jewish trade unions. Apart from its function in providing insurance, each friendly society had its own hierarchy of officers, its own rituals and its own regalia, which offered the otherwise insignificant and oppressed immigrant a sense of status in Jewish society. A leading officer could expect a gift at the time of his wedding and, on leaving office, a silver watch or an illuminated address. Each society also had its own inner social life, usually culminating in some kind of annual event: a ball perhaps, or a

Members of the Manchester branch of the Jewish Workers Circle on a picnic at Marple, c.1920. (Courtesy Manchester Jewish Museum.)

Badge worn by members of the Workers' Circle.

Regalia of the Grand Order Achei Brith Friendly Society. (Courtesy Manchester Jewish Museum.)

concert. In a sense, although not serving as places of worship, the friendly societies were the English alternative to the chevra for longer-settled and anglicising working-class Jewish families.

In 1882, only two Jewish friendly societies existed in Manchester, both designed for the higher paid Jewish worker and the emerging Jewish workshop master. The earliest was the Hebrew Sick and Burial Benefit Society, founded in 1862 by the clothing retailer Joseph Slazenger Moss. For a subscription of 4d a week, members of the society became entitled to a weekly allowance and medical attendance during illness, funeral costs and shiva benefit. In 1882 a body of workshop masters in the tailoring trade set up the Manchester Jewish Tailors' Benefit Society, of which no details survive other than that it had a membership of 140 by 1887. What amounted to an 'explosion' of Jewish friendly societies began in London in the 1880s and in Manchester in 1898, with the foundation of the Dr Herzl Lodge of what was already the London-based Grand Order of Achei Brith.

Between 1898 and 1906 five other Orders, two of them with their headquarters in Manchester, founded at least 23 lodges in the city, in addition to the emergence of 13 independent societies. The largest had over 300 members; together they comprised over 4,000. They included the Jewish Workers' Circle Friendly Society, whose members were committed to the Socialist ideology.

The friendly societies played an important role in communal history. They provided the Jewish worker with a degree of social dignity denied to him by debates around the Alien Question. They were both a symptom and a cause of the upward social mobility of the Jewish worker, expressing his improving status and protecting his material gains. They were also a clear indication of the desire of immigrants for the kinds of self-help which circumvented the charities of the Jewish middle classes.

The Jewish Benevolent Society

Other organisations with a similar purpose were the 'benevolent societies': bodies founded by the emerging Eastern European entrepreneurs to dispense charity with a generosity and discretion more in keeping with the traditional Jewish notion of Zedaka than the supposedly impersonal and investigative methods of the Jewish Board of Guardians. Austro-Hungarian and Romanian Benevolent Societies founded in the 1890s were followed in 1905 by the better known and longer-lasting Russian Jewish Benevolent Society. This was founded in April 1905 by a group of Russian immigrants attached to the tiny Bardichever Synagogue in Carnarvon Street, Cheetham, led by the insurance broker Eli Fox. One of its immediate purposes was to counter the ruling of the Jewish Board

Jewish Friendly Society regalia.

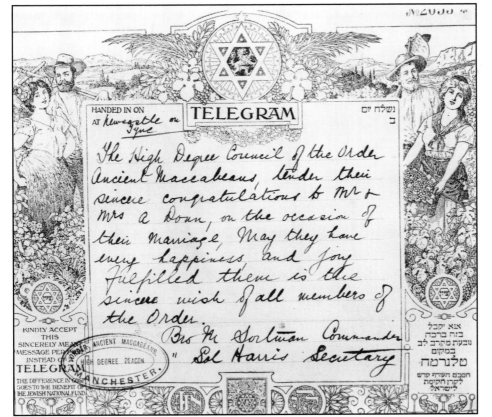

Letter of congratulations on their marriage to the Donns from the Order of Ancient Maccabeans. (Courtesy Manchester Jewish Museum.)

Members of the Order Achei Brith on a picnic, c.1920. (Courtesy Manchester Jewish Museum.)

Dora Black, a Jewish midwife, and her daughter, 1915. (Courtesy Manchester Jewish Museum.)

of Guardians that no relief could be given to an immigrant who had been in Manchester for less than six months. While having its own discreet system of assessment to identify the deserving, the society also prided itself on the secrecy of its charity: unlike those receiving aid from the Board of Guardians, the names of the recipients of support from the Benevolent Society were never revealed. Apart from immediate financial relief and small loans, the society distributed meat to poorer Jewish families at Passover. A marriage fund provided the trousseau, paid for the wedding, provided the dowry and sometimes offered accommodation to brides from poorer families who were otherwise unable to afford to marry. In 1911, when both its recipients and its subscribers had both extended well beyond families of Russian descent, the society changed its name to the Manchester Jewish Benevolent Society to become (and remain) an integral part of communal welfare: the rival and, less often, the partner of the Jewish Board of Guardians, with Eli Fox as its honorary Life President.

Chapter 8

'Rational Recreations', 1875–1914

From the late 1880s, as the verbal attack on aliens intensified, the communal elite sought to steer the immigrant poor towards institutions of leisure which would both further their anglicisation and keep them away from militant politics and from pastimes, especially gambling, which might bring the community into disrepute. In doing so, as in the case of the JLVA, they drew heavily on the models of voluntary Christian institutions equally designed to induce working-class respectability and deference.

The Jewish Working Men's Club

The first of these Christian institutions was the Working Men's Club designed by the Unitarian minister, Henry Solly, in the early 1860s to offset working-class vice, violence and political militancy and, in his own words, to bring harmony to the relationship between Capital and Labour. 'Rational [that is, orderly and sensible] relaxation and amusement,' in Solly's view, would be the first step in drawing working men towards serious intellectual and cultural pursuits,

The Manchester Jewish Working Men's Club, Southall Street, c.1890. (Courtesy Jewish Heritage UK and the Glyn family.)

Cover of the first rule book of the Jewish Working Men's Club. Only gambling, Yiddish and politics were forbidden.

Cover of the JWMC concert programme for 1921. (Courtesy Manchester Jewish Museum.)

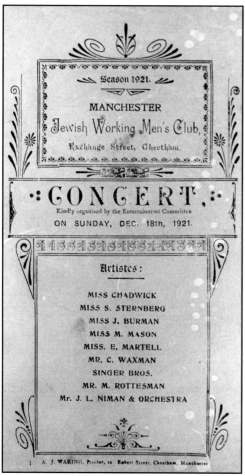

through which tension between the classes would be resolved. By 1869, 103 clubs designed for this purpose had affiliated to his Workingmen's Club and Institute Union (CIU). Throughout British Jewry, Solly's ideal club became the model for the creation of institutions of leisure which would further the respectability, placidity and Englishness of the immigrant Jewish worker. A London Jewish Working Men's Club was founded in December 1874 and, in 1883, moved into purpose-built premises in Great Alie Street, Aldgate. In 1884 a Jewish Working Men's Club and Institute was founded in Birmingham on the initiative of G.J. Emanuel, minister of the city's Singer's Hill Synagogue. In February 1887 in Manchester, at a public meeting chaired by Judah Valentine, minister of the Spanish and Portuguese Synagogue, a decision was taken to create a club: 'on a similar basis to that of London'. By March this Manchester Jewish Workingmen's Club, set up at first in rented premises, had attracted 200 members aged 16 and over, each paying 2d a week for their membership.

In a letter to the *Jewish Record*, Valentine clarified its purpose: 'Our aim is to raise the tone of our poorer brethren by instilling into them habits of industry and thrift, educating them in the language and customs of the country whither they have come to seek an asylum, and offering them light and informative entertainments in the shape of readings, dramatic and musical evenings, social gatherings where the poor man shall feel that he is at home with his brother in a higher sphere of life, in short anything that will tend to break down the barrier which just now separates class from class.' English would replace Yiddish and respectable pastimes would steer the Jewish working man away from the gambling dens of the Jewish Quarter and from political militancy symbolised by Socialist inspired Trade Unionism.

Valentine's fellow founders were drawn from a cross-section of the Jewish middle classes: English, German, Sephardi and Eastern European. They included the Sephardi cotton merchants Marco Levi and Victor Naggiar; members of long established Ashkenazi families like the optician Ben Franks (grandson of Jacob Franks); the Eastern European entrepreneurs W.L. Rothband and Nathan Laski; and the ministers of, what were then Manchester's three major synagogues, the Great, the Spanish and Portuguese and the South Manchester. In May 1887 Valentine offered the presidency to the cotton merchant Herbert Strauss, with Max Hesse and A.R. Besso as his vice-presidencies: all three were drawn from long-established and wealthy commercial families. In June 1887, with the help of a loan of £160 (perhaps from one or other of these families), the founding committee purchased a

Jenny Reece playing the part of a mill girl in James Gregson's Young Imeson, *a Yorkshire play performed at the Manchester Social Club, Manchester, in the late 1920s. (Courtesy Manchester Jewish Museum.)*

Christian social club on Cheetham Hill Road, with a dining room, concert hall, smoke room, billiard room and 'quiet room' (for draughts, cards and chess) which, on 5 June 1887, was formally opened as the Jewish Working Men's Club.

There, the club rapidly replicated the well-established activities in the London Club: classes 'for teaching elementary reading and writing to foreign Jews,' a Literary and Debating Society, a Drama Society, an Amateur Choral and Orchestral Society, a Chess Club, a Brass Band, and a series of lectures from men prominent in local and national (and chiefly non-Jewish) affairs. By 1891 the club had over 700 male members and 400 'lady associates' admitted to its activities but denied voting rights.

Part of the club's purpose, in Valentine's words, was 'to wean away our Jewish working men from the pernicious influences of places of doubtful repute'. These included the York Club, a gambling club on the corner of

The Manchester Jewish Brass Band, put together in the early days of the JWMC. (Courtesy Manchester Jewish Museum.)

Cheetham Hill Road and Carnarvon Street, set up in 1883 by two Jewish entrepreneurs, David Lazarus, then recently arrived from Liverpool, and his brother-in-law, Isaac de Costa. Although under company law the club was registered 'for the use and convenience of gentlemen in Manchester,' it soon became well-known to the police as a focus of illegal gambling. After keeping it under surveillance, under Manchester's efficient Chief of Detectives Jerome Caminada, police raided the club soon after midnight on 8 April 1888, arresting its owners and 100 men (most of them Jewish) playing solo and baccarat for money, in two front rooms. In imposing fines on the offenders, the Recorder described clubs like the York as 'immoral institutions…ruinous to families and ruinous to hard-working industrious man, and they must be put down'. Propelled into bankruptcy by the fines, Lazarus was also given a nine month gaol sentence for perjury. In what might be seen as a symbolic gesture, in June 1888 the premises of the York Club were taken over as the new (although still temporary) home of the Jewish Working Men's Club, and Strauss announced that the club had thus 'been the means of intentionally displacing two betting shops'.

During 1889–91 the JWMC, growing in membership each year, stood in opposition to the Communist/Anarchist International Workingmen's Educational Club set up in Strangeways in January 1889 by the London Jewish Socialist Leaguer, Wilhelm Wess, and which (as we have seen) inspired the creation of the first Manchester Jewish trade unions. While the International attempted to spread radical Socialism within the Manchester Jewish milieu, the

Working Men's Club set its face against such 'pestilential doctrines…subversive of government, of the family, and all that which their holy faith told them to hold dear'. It is an indication of the relatively weak influence of Socialism (as distinct from Trade Unionism) in the Jewish milieu that, while the International had become defunct by 1891, the Jewish Working Men's Club raised £2,640 to create its first purpose-built premises in Southall Street, which opened on 20 February 1892. At the opening, a banner with a portrait of the Queen was displayed beside the stage and others spanned the hall with such mottoes as 'God bless England, the land of freedom' and 'Prosperity to the Mayor.' In 1894, when the club was opened to children under 16 as junior members, its total membership exceeded 1,000; by then it had become and remained (moving to new premises as the community itself evolved) the central institution providing organised leisure activities to the community. For better or worse, it had in fact helped keep most (although not all) Jewish immigrant workers out of the reach of Socialist propagandists.

The club was also the seedbed for independent Jewish societies which, in time, were to transform the culture of the Jewish Quarter. One was the Manchester Jewish Historical Society, founded in February 1894 to mount public lectures on themes from Jewish and British history, while others included a Jewish Orchestra, a Jewish Brass Band, the Jewish Operatic Society and Manchester's first Jewish Literary Society.

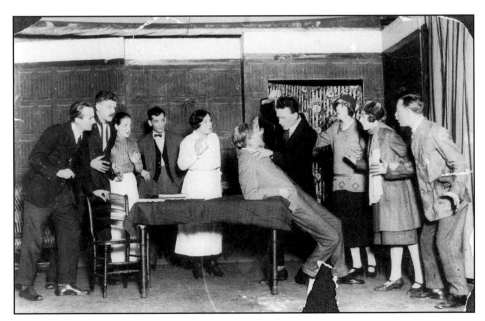

A scene from Young Imeson. *(Courtesy Manchester Jewish Museum.)*

*Chorus line of a Jewish
Operatic Society
production at the
JWMC, late 1920s.
(Courtesy Manchester
Jewish Museum.)*

The Jewish Lads' Brigade

Although it had junior members, the Jewish Working Men's Club was essentially an organisation for adult leisure. In February 1899 members of the Jewish elite, including men of both German and Eastern European origin, founded what was to become part of the upbringing of most immigrant Jewish youth: the Manchester Battalion of the Jewish Lads' Brigade (JLB), a cadet force based on the Church Lads Brigade and founded in London in 1897 by Colonel A.E. Goldsmid. It was, like the Club, an agency of social and cultural control, which sought to counter anti-alienism and protect the community by attracting the children of immigrants, after leaving school, to the customs and pastimes of English youth. Stated officially, its aim was 'to instil into the rising generation habits of usefulness, cleanliness and honour so that in learning to respect themselves they may bring credit to the community'. Within months, the Manchester JLB had attracted 300 boys. The first of its annual camps, at Lytham in August 1899, was attended by 240, housed in 50 tents, for which each boy paid 5s. By 1907, Manchester had become second only to London as a centre of JLB activity, with five companies compared to London's 19. Around 300 working-class boys were then under military instruction from an officer corps drawn from the Jewish middle classes. By 1919, 22 officers led by the commanding officer, Colonel E.C.Q. Henriques, commanded 352 boys at the JLB drill hall in Elizabeth Street, Cheetham.

In September 1907 the Brigade's management committee opened a club, the Grove House Lads Club, at 282 Bury New Road, as a social and cultural centre for the boys of the Brigade. There, they could engage every night but Friday and on Sunday afternoons, in a wide range of English leisure pursuits – table tennis, badminton, billiards, cricket, football, boxing and basketball – and were organised into teams which, in time, competed with boys from Christian clubs (with some success) for such national trophies as the Prince of Wales Boxing Shield. Only 'promiscuous card-playing' was forbidden. In such ways they were taught, in the words of the club's annual reports, 'to play the game in a clean and straightforward way' to become 'self-respecting young citizens,' a 'credit to the community' and 'worthy citizens of a great Empire'. In 1903 the Commanding Officer offered to parade before the Royal Commission on Alien Immigration 'a squad of a hundred foreign boys' which would prove how 'the children of foreign parents, after mixing with the Officers and English-born lads, assimilated English manners and customs'. Certainly, the JLB and the Working Men's Club served to ease immigrants and their children into the respectable leisure pursuits – the 'rational recreations' – of working-class England. One company of the Brigade was transformed in time into the Manchester Jewish Troop of the Boy Scout movement. Meantime, by 1897 the social gatherings established by the JLVA had evolved into a Jewish Girls' Club, which moved into Frankenburg House in 1913, after it was donated to the community by the Jewish industrialist, Isidore Frankenburg. Later, in 1916, it moved into new and larger premises at 313 Bury New Road.

Advertisement for a London Yiddish theatre group performing at the JWMC in 1900s. (Courtesy Manchester Jewish Museum.)

Colonel E.C.Q. Henriques, Commanding Officer of the Jewish Lads' Brigade, 1905. (Courtesy Manchester Jewish Museum.)

Two officers of the JLB's Manchester Battalion, 1907. (Courtesy Manchester Jewish Museum.)

Harry Cohen in the JLB, 1907. (Courtesy Manchester Jewish Museum.)

Harry Cohen and fellow members of the JLB camp at Deal, 1907. (Courtesy Manchester Jewish Museum.)

JLB officers at Prestatyn Camp. (Courtesy Manchester Jewish Museum.)

Bathing Parade at the Deal JLB Camp, 1907. (Courtesy Manchester Jewish Museum.)

Manchester JLB cricket team. (Courtesy Manchester Jewish Museum.)

JLB Award of Honour.

JLB Camp cook house, 1905. (Courtesy Manchester Jewish Museum.)

Hightown Junior Cricket Club, 1907. (Courtesy Manchester Jewish Museum.)

Grove House Harriers, 1913. (Courtesy Manchester Jewish Museum.)

Grove House Lads' cricket team. (Courtesy Manchester Jewish Museum.)

Grove House Lads' football team 1924–25. (Courtesy Manchester Jewish Museum.)

Christmas at Joseph Mandelberg's waterproof garment factory, the Albion Works in Salford. (Courtesy Manchester Jewish Museum.)

Bessie Cohen, the daughter of a Manchester immigrant family, who became one of the first 'Tiller Girls', a group first formed in Manchester in the 1890s.

Heaton Park in 1918. Situated to the immediate north of the Jewish Quarter, the park became an important meeting place for Jewish families from Cheetham Hill.

Lawrence Demmy, a Jewish ice dancing champion and subsequently an Olympic judge, who learnt his skating at the Manchester Ice Palace, with his partner, Jean Westwood.

The Manchester Ice Palace, established in Derby Street, Cheetham Hill in 1910. The world ice dancing championships were held there in 1911. It was a favoured social and sporting venue for members of Jewish families living in the area. This listed building still exists, although it is now a warehouse and has been shorn of its original white marble covering.

Interior of the Manchester Ice Palace, 1910.

Succah at the Manchester Jews' School, c.1917. (Courtesy Manchester Jewish Museum.)

ABOVE RIGHT: Class at the Southall Street Board School, 1924. (Courtesy Manchester Jewish Museum.)

Class at the Waterloo Road Board School, c.1923. (Courtesy Manchester Jewish Museum.)

Jews in Christian Schools

By this time, the Manchester Jews' School had long since proved too small to accommodate the immigrant child population. Immigrant children were to be found in many of the Christian voluntary schools in the Cheetham area, such as St John's Church of England School in Hightown, and in the two Board Schools of Southall Street and Waterloo Road (opened in 1889), created under the Education Act of 1870. Waterloo Road and Southall Street, in particular,

Winners of 27 scholarships from Standard 7 of the Southall Street Board School, 1916. (Courtesy Manchester Jewish Museum.)

Southall Street Board School.

became in all but name the 'Jews' Schools'. Their meals were kosher, their headmasters were Jewish and the school calendars took into account the Jewish Sabbath and Holy Days. It is said that, on Jewish holy days, so few children remained at Southall Street that the whole school closed down. So wide was this dispersal of Jewish children that, in 1901, a Jewish Religious Education Board was set up to provide religious instruction in Christian schools with Jewish pupils. The informal body, which in 1916 arranged for 69 Jewish boys, chiefly from the Southall and Waterloo Road schools, to be sent to a camp for one week in Kettleshulme, emerged in the following years as the Manchester School Camps Association, which acquired its own permanent campsite at Prestatyn in 1923, to which between 600 and 800 children (some of them non-Jewish) were sent in groups of 50 from 12 Manchester schools for one week during the summer months.

A scene from Israel in the Kitchen, a play by Noah Epstein, performed by the Manchester Jewish Literary Society in Manchester's Lesser Free Trade Hall in the 1920s. (Courtesy Manchester Jewish Museum.)

Jewish Literary Societies

The children of the orthodox Jewish middle classes of Eastern European origin who were rarely sent to the proletarian Jews' School, to Christian primary schools or to the new Board Schools, typically progressed from private schools and tutors to Manchester Grammar School, Manchester High School for Girls or their lesser equivalents, and on into their fathers' businesses, British universities and the Liberal professions. From the late 1890s there evolved, chiefly in the Higher Broughton area at first, Jewish cultural and sporting societies designed by the parental generation to introduce such children, in a 'safe' Jewish setting, to the pastimes and social niceties of the English middle classes. Among them were literary societies which, on the English model, mixed social activities and entertainments with discussions, lectures and debates centred on the issues of the day. The longest lasting of these in Manchester was the Jewish Literary and Social Union founded in 1903 by, among others, the Jewish textile dealer and calico printer Samuel Finburgh, and meeting from 1904 at the Athenaeum, a major focus of the cultural activities of the non-Jewish middle class. Smaller Jewish literary societies, more socially diverse in their memberships, flourished in Edwardian Manchester, many attached to friendly societies and synagogues. Apart from their (largely successful) anglicising programmes, literary societies provided many aspiring young Jews, including Finburgh, Sidney Hamburger and Michael Fidler, with their first experience of British politics. It also allowed talented immigrants, like the painter Emmanuel Levy, the dramatist and poet Hymie Gouldman, and the novelist Maisie Mosco (who centred her *Almonds and Raisins* trilogy on Manchester), with their earliest creative opportunities.

The Manchester Jewish Literary Society, Christmas 1938. (Courtesy Manchester Jewish Museum.)

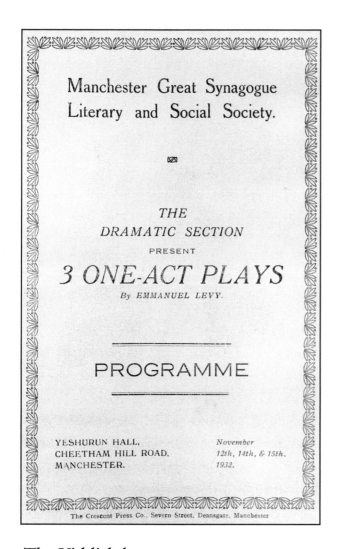

The Crescent Press Co., Severn Street, Deansgate, Manchester

Frontispiece of a programme of one-act plays by Emmanuel Levy, performed by the Manchester Great Synagogue Literary and Social Society in the Synagogues's Yeshurun Hall, 1932. Emmanuel Levy, from a Manchester Jewish immigrant family, was also an impressionist painter of national note. (Courtesy Manchester Jewish Museum.)

Programme for The Quaker Girl, performed by the Manchester Jewish Amateur Operatic Society at Salford's Palace Theatre in February 1923. (Courtesy Manchester Jewish Museum.)

The Yiddish language

Although such anglicising mechanisms as the Jews' School, the JLVA, the JWMC, the JLB and the literary societies effectively crushed Yiddish as the first spoken language of the second generation, they did not at first eliminate Yiddish culture in all its forms. Yiddish newspapers were available from London and New York, although the attempt to start one in Manchester failed. Yiddish theatre groups, most of them American, toured the country putting on Yiddish plays in Manchester and other centres of Jewish population. Jewish newsagents, at least before World War One, often housed circulating libraries which included books in Yiddish. Harris Segal, whose shop in Moreton Street, Strangeways, sold 'school books,

The Red Rose cricket team, a Jewish team which played on a ground near Elizabeth Street. (Courtesy Manchester Jewish Museum.)

Jewish football team, Manchester 1913. (Courtesy Manchester Jewish Museum.)

Ladies waiting to take tea at the Manchester Jewish Tennis Club in Higher Broughton, c.1890. (Courtesy Manchester Jewish Museum.)

dictionaries, newspapers, sheet music, stationery, toys, dominoes, playing cards, draughts, lotto, prayer shawls, ritual items and pieces of embroider', boasted also of holding 'the largest library in Manchester for reading books'. Among the books in his library were thin weekly parts of tracts, novels and magazines (some of which have survived by chance), which could be borrowed for a penny a book. Some of these were religious homilies. Most were the weekly extracts of Yiddish novels published in New York between 1894 and 1897, with such titles as *The Secrets of Paris, The Tyrannical Mother, The Lady Poisoner* and *The Innocent Companion of the Vampire.*

Nor can the propaganda of the Jewish elite be said to have weaned all families of Eastern European origin off radical politics or less reputable pastimes. Gambling remained the predominant vice of the working-class Jewish Quarter with left-wing politics as its major ideology. In 1904 a Cheetham Clarion Fellowship was founded as a Jewish branch of Robert Blatchford's Socialist Clarion Movement.

A line of continuity could be drawn between the Jewish radical Trade Unionism of the first decades of the 20th century and the Jewish Communists, like the young Frank Allaun, who fought Mosley's fascists in the 1930s.

Chapter 9

The First Zionists, 1885–1914

Another political tradition which flourished in Manchester was Zionism. Since the exile, the hope of a Jewish return to the Holy Land had been enshrined in the prayers and ritual of Orthodox Judaism. This was largely interpreted by the Jews of the Diaspora, including those of Manchester, in transcendental terms; at some unknown, but probably distant, point in the future, a Return would be part of a divinely ordained Redemption under the aegis of the Messiah. There had always been a tiny minority, however, for whom settlement in Palestine, then part of the Ottoman Empire, was seen as a prior means of developing a unique relationship with the Eternal. For other pious Jews, Palestine came to represent an escape from what was seen as the dangerously corrosive forces unleashed by emancipation. For these reasons, the tiny Jewish population which Palestine had always housed was continuously replenished. By the beginning of the 19th century there were perhaps 10,000 Jews in a total Palestinian population estimated at between 150,000 and 300,000. During the first half of the 19th century, Jewish philanthropists (particularly from the Montefiore and Rothschild families) had given some shape to this sporadic resettlement by the planting of agricultural colonies. A small but steady stream of Russian immigrants, suffering under the anti-Jewish policies of the Tsar, made their way to the Holy Land, particularly after the easing of Ottoman discrimination against non-Muslims after 1856.

Manchester Jewry and Palestine

Manchester Jewry's first contact with Palestine took the form of 'haluka': money collected in the city and distributed to Palestinian Jews dependent for survival on such outside aid. During the 1860s

Zion Hall, 97 Cheetham Hill Road, the headquarters of the Manchester Zionist Association, c.1890. The building also housed the Shechita Board, which supervised the production of kosher meat. (Courtesy Jewish Heritage UK and the Glyn family.)

and 1870s David Meyer Isaacs, minister of the Manchester Great Synagogue, was president of a Jerusalem Society founded for such a purpose. In 1878 the Russian immigrant optician, William Aronsberg, succeeded Isaacs as president of what had by then become known as the Manchester Society for the Relief of the Poor Perushim. There is record of his personal appeal in October 1879, after which funds were despatched to Palestine through the British Consul.

Jewish Colonisation Societies

It was not until the early 1880s, however, following the penal May Laws in Tsarist Russia, that evidence exists of a Manchester movement to actually promote the colonisation of Palestine. In March 1882 Rabbi Dr Berendt Salomon, the Danish minister of the Manchester Great Synagogue, wrote a strong letter to the *Jewish Chronicle* to suggest that Palestine was a more fitting destination than the United States for Jewish immigrants from Russia. He explained that Jewish immigrants to the US risked provoking anti-Jewish feeling without finding material security. He imagined Jewish families strolling through the streets of American cities 'scarcely knowing where to look for the next day's meal'. In Palestine, on the other hand, where liberal donations from the West might promote economic progress, 'all the persecuted Jews would find a true fatherland'. Salomon's was a lone Manchester voice. Probably of greater influence was the creation in Russia in December 1884 of Chovovei Zion (the Lovers of Zion), to promote Russian immigrant participation in the more systematic colonisation of Palestine.

The ripples which flowed from Kattowitz, where Chovovei Zion (CZ) was founded, included the setting up of a Manchester Society for the Promotion of the Colonisation of Palestine at some time during the autumn of 1885. Said to have then found support 'among the humble Jews of Manchester', its president was the Russian immigrant cap-making entrepreneur, Mark Doniger. A public meeting chaired by Judah Valentine, in September 1885, 'to elicit the sympathy and advice of the leading members of the Manchester community' suggests, however, that the 'humble' felt in need of more influential support. When this was not forthcoming,

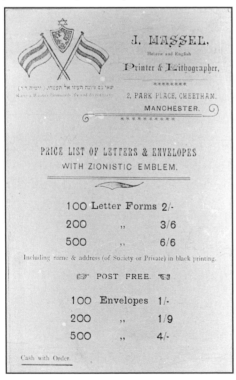

Advert for Zionist stationery supplied by the printing firm of Joseph Massel at 2 Park Place, Cheetham. (Courtesy Manchester Jewish Museum.)

the society appears to have disbanded. For the next five years, interest in Palestine was again confined to the raising of haluka, particularly by Louis Jacobs, the energetic secretary of the Manchester Talmud Torah, and Susman Cohen, then rising to prominence as the fiery minister of a chevra in Red Bank. During 1887, both delivered public lectures on the needs of the 'distressed Jewish poor' of Jerusalem. In a letter to the *Jewish Record* in July 1887, Jacobs made an impassioned plea for help from the Diaspora in establishing factories in Jerusalem. He believed Jewish settlers in the Holy Land were no longer to be seen only as 'vulnerable learned men' who had chosen to devote their lives to study; the majority were now 'men, young and middle-aged, though they spend some hours in study, employ the most part of the day in endeavours to make a living'. They required help, which they could not expect from the Ottoman authorities, in furthering the industrial and agricultural development of Palestine.

Jacobs's stress on the practical value of colonisation was timely. In May 1890 the Chovovei Zion Association of Britain was founded in London by Colonel A.E.W. Goldsmid to support the settlement in Palestine of Russo-Jewish emigrants. In August 1890 two of its members, its chairman Ben-Elihu Rubinstein and the charismatic preacher, Revd H.Z. Maccoby, the so-called Kamenitzer Magid, visited Manchester at the invitation of the Manchester New Synagogue, where a meeting chaired by Louis Jacobs initiated the Manchester branch with an initial membership of 160. In Manchester, Chovovei Zion found fertile soil, particularly at first among

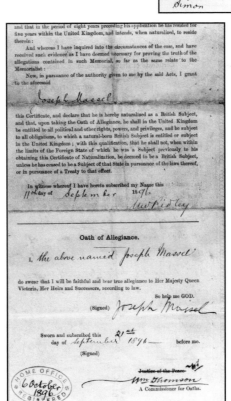

Naturalisation papers of the Manchester Zionist Joseph Massel, page 1 and 2. (Courtesy Manchester Jewish Museum.)

1 Ben Elial 2 Joseph Massel 3 Isaac Chagan
4 J.B. Herwald 5 Lewis Lexensohn 6 a Gordon
Manchester delegates to the first English Zionist
Federation conference June 8th 1899

Manchester delegates to the first conference of the English Zionists Federation, 1899. (Courtesy Manchester Jewish Museum.)

Members of the Daughters of Zion at a Palestine Bazaar in Manchester in 1932. (Courtesy Manchester Jewish Museum.)

the immigrant nouveaux riche. A mass meeting of the branch was held in January 1891 at the Romanian Synagogue in Strangeways. A month later, the entry of a young Sephardi merchant and financier, Barrow Belisha, into the society marked the beginning of wider support from the Jewish middle classes. Belisha brought other Sephardi merchants with him; from the Reform Synagogue came its minister Lawrence Simmons and the cotton merchant E.M. Henriques; from the Great Synagogue, Berendt Salomon. Other Eastern European entrepreneurs who had joined by the end of 1892 included Nathan Laski, his brother Morris (now linked in the cotton exporting firm, Laski and Laski) and the waterproof garment manufacturers, Philip Frankenstein and Isidore Frankenburg. By then, membership of the Manchester branch had risen to over 450, over half the total membership of the English movement.

Although the words 'nation' and 'nationality' were bandied about at Chovovei Zion meetings and Goldsmid related his movement to 'the universal uprising of the national spirit among the peoples of the earth', the aim was colonisation, not statehood. In particular, Chovovei Zion saw itself as the means by which Russian Jewish emigrants would be diverted from Britain. 'What was wanted', Barrow Belisha told one meeting, 'was that their persecuted co-religionists in Russia, instead of having to come to overcrowded towns in this and other countries, should go back to Palestine.' It was for this reason that colonisation achieved such support from the Jewish elite: it was an alternative to anglicisation. In January 1894 the Manchester Great Synagogue mounted a service attended by 1,500 people to be addressed by Colonel

Goldsmid. He told the congregants that Chovovei Zion was the 'political centre' from which the otherwise helpless Jews of Russia might make their appeal heard and through which they might attain settlement in Palestine.

Working-class Zionism

What was missing from the Chovovei Zion 'tent' in Manchester was a following from the Jewish immigrant working class, increasingly suspicious of the intentions of their Jewish betters. Frustrated, too, by the absence of any marked religious component in Chovovei Zion's ideals, and by the 'Englishness' of its meetings, Yiddish-speaking proletarian Jews began to take initiatives of their own. The first, during the summer of 1891, was Bnei Zion (the Sons of Zion) which, beginning at a meeting in the Talmud Torah, went on to rent what had been a conversionist mission hall in Briddon Street, Strangeways, as an office, library and venue for lectures and debates. Although small in numbers (it had only 20 members) and fragile (it lasted for less than a year), Bnei Zion marks the small beginnings of a transition in Manchester from the 'philanthropic Zionism,' created and led by an anglicised middle-class elite, to a movement rooted in the spontaneous idealism of working-class immigrant Jewry. It was followed by another grass-roots organisation, Agudath Achim (the

Friendly Society medallion inscribed 'Order of Ancient Maccabeans Grand Beacon.' The Order of Maccabeans was a Zionist Friendly Society with several branches, or 'beacons,' in Manchester. (Courtesy Manchester Jewish Museum.)

Children at the cheder (Hebrew school) of Isaiah Wassilevsky in Cheetham Hill. Wassilevsky was a strong Zionist and a pioneer in the movement for the creation of modern Hebrew. (Courtesy Manchester Jewish Museum.)

Portrait of Joseph Massel from a history of Hebrew poets. Apart from his printing and his Zionism, Massel wrote poems in Hebrew, including one commemorating the Silver Jubilee of Queen Victoria. (Courtesy Manchester Jewish Museum.)

United Brethren), founded by 18 young men in the summer of 1892 'to settle themselves in Palestine as colonists'. As soon as the cumulative contributions of its members (at 2s 6d each a week) were sufficient, one of its members, a Mr J. Yablonsky, was despatched to Palestine in an attempt to buy land for a settlement from the Ottoman Government. When this proved impossible, according to one of the members: 'we had no alternative except to wind up the society. All monies were distributed among the members'.

Finally, on 30 March 1894, T.B. Herwald, a waterproof garment worker who had belonged to both earlier societies (and for a time to Chovovei Zion) called together 15 young fellow workers to create what he saw as a more vigorous society, Dorshei Zion (the Seekers for Zion). By the end of the year, with 10 additional members, Dorshei Zion rented premises at 41 Cheetham Hill Road as its library and meeting place. It was a struggle, as Herwald remembered: 'On many occasions we went on a house-to-house canvass collecting money.' Such was the popular indifference to Zionism at this stage that, when asked for whom they were collecting, they answered 'for a poor Jewish family'. 'I think we were not misrepresenting the facts', Herwald wrote later, 'as the Jewish people are the poorest among nations.'

It was Dorshei Zion which served as a bridge between movements for the colonisation of Palestine and a 'new Zionism', which also sought the recreation of a Jewish *state* envisaged by the Austrian Theodore Herzl in his *Judenstaat*, published in Vienna in 1896. Throughout the Jewish world, Herzl's ideals were a turning point in the history of Zionism, as colonisation gave way to preparations for the creation of a Jewish nation. In Manchester, following Herzl's visit to London in July 1896, according to Herwald: 'the whole Dorshei Zion was newly born and they immediately became adherents of Herzl and proclaimed him their leader'. In the light of this new objective, Chovovei Zion gave way to a galaxy of political organisations held together by annual 'congresses', the first in Basle in 1897.

Not everyone embraced Herzl's political aspirations. There were those who feared that it would give rise to accusations of exclusivity or divided loyalties. Barrow Belisha, son of Isaac David Belisha, saw Herzlian Zionists as 'Jewish Fenians'. Others believed that it would reverse the processes of acculturation and integration into the nations of Jewish residence on which the security of the Jewish people was based. Nathan Laski, who had always held this view, now held back from committing himself to Herzl's view of the Jewish future. One Manchester speaker commented: 'Our salvation lay in our dispersal, in virtue of which anti-Semitic attack can never reach us in one body.' Others continued to believe that Zionism of any kind constituted a sacrilegious anticipation of the coming of the Messiah. Although Zionist formations now multiplied in Manchester, it was not until after World War Two that Zionism can be said to have taken hold of the community as a whole.

VI. Zionisten-Kongress in Basel
23. bis 28. August 1903

DELEGIERTEN-KARTE

Invitation to Joseph Massel to represent Manchester at the Sixth Zionist Congress in Basle. (Courtesy Manchester Jewish Museum.)

Dorshei Zion (DZ), under the presidency of Joseph Massel, a Russian immigrant printer who had arrived in Manchester in the early 1890s, was the epicentre of this initial institutional explosion. DZ itself became the focus of propaganda for Herzl's 'Basle programme'. In May 1902 it moved to 97 Cheetham Hill Road which, as Zion Hall, became and remained for over 40 years the centre for the coordination of Zionist activity by a Manchester Zionist Association. Around it, by 1904, there were at least 12 other Zionist organisations, including three for the young; one for 'working men', with its headquarters in the (Jewish) Labour Hall in Strangeways; two devoted to fundraising; the first Manchester branch (or 'Beacon') of the Zionist Friendly Society, the Order of Ancient Maccabeans; a Hebrew Speaking Society founded by the *cheder* teacher Isaiah Wassilevsky and devoted to the revival of Hebrew as a spoken (and national) language; a religious Zionist group, committed to creating a Jewish state on a religious basis; and another, the Daughters of Zion, created in March 1900 by and for Jewish women. Their total membership was perhaps 500, but as one contemporary commented: 'what was lacking in numbers was compensated by the intense interest in speculative discussion'. In March 1903 representatives from seven other provincial communities met in Manchester to form themselves into the District Committee of the English Zionist Federation. Manchester was on the way to becoming 'the capital of English Zionism'.

Chaim Weitzmann and wife, Vera, in Manchester, c.1910. (Courtesy Manchester Jewish Museum.)

BOTTOM RIGHT: Committee meeting of the Manchester Zionist Association, c.1920. (Courtesy Manchester Jewish Museum.)

The first national executive of the Women's International Zionist Organisation, London, c.1920. (Courtesy Manchester Jewish Museum.)

Weitzmann in Manchester

In 1904 Chaim Weitzmann, a man of Russian birth and already an important figure in international Zionism, arrived in Manchester from Zurich to take up a post in the chemistry department at the University of Manchester. He was met at the station by Joseph Massel, in whose house he spent his first days in the city and through whom he made his first Zionist contacts. Throwing himself into local Zionist activity, while keeping in contact with the international movement, it was in Manchester that he built around himself a body of influential supporters, Jewish and non-Jewish, which included, on the Jewish side, Massel, Simon Marks and Israel Sieff, the joint managing directors of Marks and Spencer; Dr Charles Dreyfus, owner of the Clayton Aniline Dye Company and a Conservative city councillor; Leon Simon, the son of the minister of the South Manchester Synagogue; Harry Dagut, the teacher-son of an immigrant Rabbi Mendel Dagutski; Harry Sacher, a leader writer with the *Manchester Guardian;* the Hebrew book seller and 'Commander' of the Mount Horeb Beacon of the Order of Ancient Maccabeans, Isaac Chazan; the Sephardi merchant, Samuel J. Cohen and, on the non-Jewish side, the *Manchester Guardian's* editor, C.P. Scott; his colleagues, Herbert Sidebotham and Walter Crozier; and the Conservative MP for East Manchester, A.J. Balfour. It was Marks, Sieff, Simon and Dagut who in 1911 came together with Joseph Massel's son, Simon, to create the monthly *Zionist Banner*, one of the first Zionist periodicals in England.

It was largely through this Manchester School of Zionists and through the contacts he had made in the city that in 1917, after leaving Manchester for

London, that Weitzmann was able to persuade
the British Government, in which Balfour was
then Foreign Secretary, to issue, in November
1917, the Balfour Declaration, committing itself
to support for a 'Jewish homeland in Palestine'.
It was the Balfour Declaration, in turn, which
provided a realistic basis for the creation of the
Jewish State in what, in 1918, had become the
British Mandate of Palestine.

Zionist Movements

Locally, meantime, the differing segments of the Zionist movement had all
taken root. Mizrachi Zionism, which looked forward to a Jewish state based
on Talmudic Judaism, had reached Manchester before December 1918 when
Israel Yoffey, Rabbi of the Manchester Central Synagogue since 1897,
convened the first national conference of the movement in the city. A branch
of Poale Zion, the Zionist workers' movement, was established in Manchester
by April 1906. In that same year Marie de Picciotto, born in Aleppo in 1882
into an important Sephardi family, arrived in Manchester. Already a
convinced Zionist, after attending the Manchester High School for Girls she
joined the Daughters of Zion at about the same time as Michel Marks's
daughter Rebecca, also a former pupil of the High School. Together they
turned the Daughters of Zion into a major vehicle for advancing women's
membership of the Zionist movement. It was Rebecca Marks who, with
Helena Weissberg, a teacher at the Manchester Jews' School and another
member of the Daughters of Zion, was a leading figure in the establishment
of the Federation of Zionist Women in 1919. Subsequently, the initial
discussions which led to the foundation of the Women's International Zionist
Organisation (WIZO) in 1920, now with branches throughout the Jewish
world, were held in the house in Belfield Road, Didsbury, into which Rebecca
had moved after her marriage to her fellow Zionist, Israel Sieff. Marie de
Picciotto (after her marriage to a Sephardi cotton merchant, Marie Nahum,
in 1913) remained in Manchester as the leading figure in women's Zionism.

*Members of the
Manchester Zionist
Association, c.1920. The
secretary, Eva Black, is
on the right. (Courtesy
Manchester Jewish
Museum.)*

*Israel Wiener, an early
member of the workers'
Zionist organisation,
Poale Zion. (Courtesy
Manchester Jewish
Museum.)*

Chapter 10

The Impact of World War One

Alec Coleman and Solomon Weinstein of Manchester in France during World War One. (Courtesy Manchester Jewish Museum.)

Jack White, who won the Victoria Cross for bravery during World War One. (Courtesy Manchester Jewish Museum.)

World War One was an important turning point in the history of the community. The processes of anglicisation were furthered by the engagement of Jewish volunteers and conscripts in the theatres of war. These processes included some arising from the informal mixing of immigrant Jewish families with their Christian neighbours and from their casual involvement in the life of the city, while others were pressed upon the immigrants by the Jewish middle classes or by English trade unionists. The Jewish young entered the armed services on a scale which exceeded that of British society as a whole. Many were wounded or killed. One of them, the Mancunian Jack White, a former member of the JLB, was awarded the Victoria Cross. War contracts, for groundsheets and uniforms, helped cement the prosperity of rising immigrant industries. The war was equally the beginning of a fight-back by those Orthodox and observant Jews who feared that anglicisation had proceeded so far as to threaten the 'traditional Judaism' of a younger generation. The internment by the British Government of Jews of German, Austrian, Romanian and Turkish nationality (judged to be enemy aliens) and attacks on Jewish aliens for supposedly evading military service also suggested to the community's leaders, the need for some organisation which might represent, give voice to and protect the interests of the community as a whole. Finally, the years of war and its immediate aftermath saw the completion of the community's comprehensive system of welfare.

The Jewish Representative Council

Until 1919, the community had two agencies with a brief which extended over the community as a whole: the Shechita Board and the Beth Din. Although the Board was formally concerned only with the mechanisms for the provision of kosher meat, and the Beth Din with the settlement of issues related to Jewish law, the Board had, in practice, come to see itself by 1914 as a forum for the debate and settlement of secular disputes and as the means by which the community mediated with the wider society.

The beginning of a movement towards a secular unifying body came in February 1915 when a temporary 'Communal Committee', representing all Manchester's Jewish institutions, was set up to collect funds for Polish and Palestinian Jews suffering from the outbreak of war. The imperative of unity was reinforced by a perceived need to protect those threatened with internment as enemy aliens and to keep the Zionist flame alive during the years of war. On 27 January 1916 at a meeting of like-minded men, most of them Zionists, at the house of Nahum Isaac Adler in Heywood Street, Cheetham, it was decided to create a Manchester Jewish National and Communal Council, this time with the object of 'representing and protecting all Jewish national interests within and without the Community and to interest itself in all Jewish institutions in Manchester'. The pressure, it may be presumed, came chiefly from Zionists not represented either nationally on the London *Board of Deputies* or locally on the Shechita Board, both made up only of delegates from synagogues. This first Communal Council, chaired by T.B. Herwald, included representatives not only from Zionist formations, but from Friendly Societies, Trade Unions, literary societies and other communal institutions, all denied any place in the governance of national or local Jewry, both dominated by 'self-appointed leaders', many of them, like Nathan Laski in Manchester, non-Zionist.

Temporary marker of the grave of Captain E.C. Simon, 5th Lancashire Fusiliers, killed in action on 17 August 1915.

Not everyone in Manchester favoured a council so inclusive, or one with such Zionist overtones. Within weeks the Shechita Board came up with the idea of a 'permanent communal organisation' made up of representatives of synagogues and other religious organisations, while the community's informal oligarchs, notably the Sephardi merchant David Garson and Nathan Laski, favoured a central committee made up of Manchester's delegates to the Board of Deputies, of whom Laski was one, with a few co-opted additions. Meantime, in December 1916, the National and Communal Council changed its name to the Manchester Jewish Representative Council and broadened its remit to include 'the safeguarding of the interests of the Jewish community of Manchester and Salford in everything appertaining to its affairs within and without from a Jewish point of view'. Throughout 1917, competition (described by one observer as 'fratricidal strife') persisted between three organisations, each claiming to represent the community in discussions, for

*Nathan Laski and his
family in the grounds of
his house in Smedley
Lane, Cheetham Hill.
(Courtesy Manchester
Jewish Museum.)*

*Fireman's tobacconists
shop in Cheetham Hill.
(Courtesy Manchester
Jewish Museum.)*

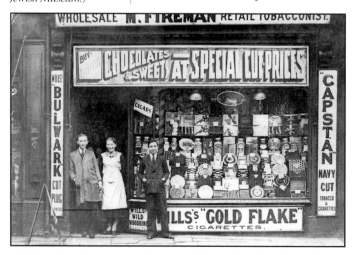

example, over war-time difficulties in the supply and price of Jewish dietary requirements, Sabbath observance and children's education, around a Government threat (actually carried out in August 1917) to deport to Russia those Russian-Jewish aliens (that is, non-naturalised immigrants of Russian origin) who would not agree to their conscription into the British army, and about the implications of the Balfour Declaration (made on 2 November 1917).

Unanimity was restored only by a series of fraught discussions and compromises which culminated on 1 February 1919 in a meeting of delegates from 18 synagogues and 12 Friendly Societies, under the chairmanship of Edward Henry Langdon, to discuss the formation of a Council of Manchester and Salford Jews. Agreement was reached, and the inaugural meeting of the Council was held on 7 February in the library of the Jewish Working Men's Club. With an annually elected president (the first was Langdon) and an executive committee, the expectation (embodied in a formal constitution) was that the council would serve as the sole mouthpiece of the community, that it would protect the community from anti-Semitic abuse, and that it would serve to promote harmony among the community's many institutions. Its president would be seen as the community's lay leader, its expenses met by assessed contributions from its constituents, its business transacted by weekly meetings of its executive and by plenary monthly meetings. Similar trains of events in these same years generated similar councils in the Jewish communities of Leeds and Glasgow.

They cannot properly be described as communal parliaments since they possessed no legislative function or coercive powers which made their decisions mandatory. They served chiefly as the forums for the discussion of communal matters and as intermediaries between the Jewish community and the wider society. In Manchester, it was only under the presidency of such strong-minded and charismatic figures as Nathan Laski (1935–41) that the council could make its writ run throughout the community.

Laski, in fact, exercised greater personal power over the community than anyone before or since; his obituarist in the local Jewish press described him as 'King' of the Manchester Jews. It was said that his late arrival at a communal meeting could overturn a decision otherwise unanimously agreed. Council presidents, whose influence was exerted only by consensus, have generally reflected the makeup of the communal majority: all but one have been Orthodox, all have been Zionists, most have been businessmen (or since 1980, when the first woman president was elected, businesswomen). Since mediation was their major function, all were seen to have status within both the minority and majority communities.

Sarah Silver outside G. Rosenberg's Dairy, 40 Waterloo Road, c.1920. (Courtesy Manchester Jewish Museum.)

The Napoo Gang

The setting up of the Jewish Representative Council was an official means of countering external threats to the Jewish community. Such threats, however, also had their origin in a working-class Manchester untouched by officialdom. At some time in late 1915 or early 1916, among the many street gangs of Manchester there appeared one, in Butler Street, Ancoats, which called itself 'the Napoo Gang'. Its title came from a World War One slang word meaning 'vanished, gone for ever'. Apart from the street wars with rivals which were the regular activities of Manchester gangs, the Napoo were distinctive in that they targeted, in particular, Jews of their own age that they encountered on the streets of the Jewish Quarter, across the Irk from Ancoats, and young women (of any religion) whom they would stalk and whose long hair they would cut off.

Conscription had recently been introduced and these young Napoo boys, aged 15 and 16, were aware that their time would come for

Three members of the Rosenberg family outside their dairy in Waterloo Road. (Courtesy Manchester Jewish Museum.)

service on what were by then well-known to be the dangerous war fronts. One interpretation of their selected victims is that they were young people who were seen to be escaping conscription; those Jewish boys who, as aliens, would not be liable for conscription, and young girls of their own age. Their attacks were generated, it might be argued, by anger at their own perceived fate and at those who supposedly were to escape it. The fact that Jewish boys born in Britain would be conscripted, and that many aliens served as volunteers, escaped their notice.

The Napoo Gang did not, however, escape the notice of Jewish soldiers returning to Manchester on leave from the Western Front. Feeling insulted, in 1917 a group of Jewish soldiers on leave decided to put an end to it. Returning to the garment factories in which they had once worked, they collected shears and rollers and crossed the Irk with them to meet the Napoo boys on their own ground. Tradition has it that a pitched battle in Ancoats, near Jewish New Year 1917, saw the Napoo defeated to the extent that they never appeared again.

The Lusitania Riots

The sinking of the American passenger ship, the *Lusitania*, by a German submarine in May 1915 caused a huge loss of civilian lives, including women and children, sparking off anti-German riots in many British cities, including Manchester and Salford. Crowds gathered on the streets and stoned the shops of German pork butchers and other shops with names thought to be German. In many instances this included shops with foreign names which were in fact Jewish rather than German. Typically, one member of the crowd would lead the way by hurling a stone at a shop window and the mob would follow by ransacking the premises.

Henry Grant, a young Jewish boy, came across a crowd on Lower Broughton Road in Salford behaving in exactly this way. He watched with growing anger as the mob ransacked shops with foreign names, including those he knew to be Jewish. He noticed that a Christian tobacconist with a very English name was leaning nonchalantly on his shop door, smirking at the violence. This made up his mind. Picking up a stone at the back of the crowd he hurled it at the window of the tobacconist. Immediately the crowd moved in and within minutes the tobacconist's stock had been stolen or destroyed.

On another level, the riots persuaded many Germans, including German Jews, that the time had come to either leave, change their names or place notes in their shop windows advertising their patriotism.

The German community which had done so much for Manchester was decimated. Never again were people of German origin, whether Christian or Jewish, to play such important roles in Manchester society.

The Sinai League

One of the earliest Orthodox Jewish reactions to the risks of excessive anglicisation was the founding in 1916 of a Manchester branch of the London-based Sinai League, a youth section of the *haredi* Aguda Yisroel, by Revd A.M. Adler, the minister of Manchester's Romanian Synagogue. Finally accommodated at Sinai House at 36 Elizabeth Street, the Sinai League was in many ways an orthodox alternative to the JLB and the Grove House Lads' Club. While it did organise sporting activities, its central purpose was 'to preserve and promote Traditional Judaism among Jewish youth'. In its Beth Hamedrash, with its library and reading room, there were facilities for regular religious services and for the traditional celebration of the Jewish festivals. In 'a true Jewish atmosphere', classes, lectures and debates sought to reinforce the allegiance of the young to 'authentic Judaism'. When the League branch in Manchester collapsed in 1925, itself an indication of the religious alienation of the Jewish young, Israel Slotki did his best, against the odds of assimilation and the multiplication of secular amusements, to set up Jewish Study Circles.

The Delamere Home

World War One, with its destruction of so many young men, also served to emphasise the need to protect the health of the next generation of Jewish children.

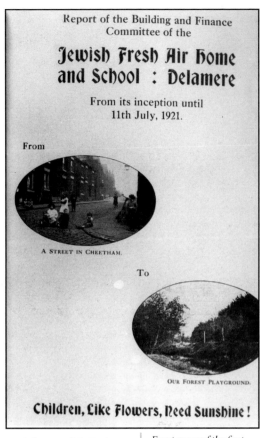

Front cover of the first annual report of the Delamere Fresh Air Home for Delicate (Jewish) Children.

Collecting tin for the Delamere Home. (Courtesy Manchester Jewish Museum.)

Children working in the flower and vegetable gardens of the Delamere Home. (Courtesy Manchester Jewish Museum.)

In 1920, as concern grew in the community for the health of children brought up in the Jewish slums, a movement was launched by middle-class Jewish philanthropists for the replacement of the holiday home established by the JLVA in Chinley by a residential Jewish Fresh Air Home and School for Delicate Manchester and Salford Children. The aim was to provide an education and a cure, in healthy rural surroundings, for children suffering from 'any of the complaints which result from the neglect of delicacy in children: specifically, anaemia, rheumatism and tuberculosis'. Under the motto 'Children – like flowers – need Sunlight', an appeal was launched under the chairmanship of Dorothy Quas-Cohen, the wife of a waterproof garment manufacturer, for £40,000 to build such a home in Delamere Forest in Cheshire, and to pay the salaries of two resident teachers and a trained nurse. Following its success, the home opened in 1921 for 40 children, 20 boys and 20 girls, from families living in Red Bank, Strangeways and Lower Broughton. It marked too, an important stage in the career of Manchester's leading woman philanthropist, Margaret Langdon, the daughter of the cotton merchant Edward Henry Langdon. She graduated from volunteer work with the JLVA to become the home's honorary secretary and leading activist.

It was Margaret Langdon who, recognising that 'there was no Convalescent Home that would admit both a mother and her baby', was the inspiration behind the foundation in 1928 of a Jewish Holiday Home for Mothers and Babies at Rose Bank, Lymm, some five miles south of Manchester. At its opening in July 1928 it was described as a 'commodious' and 'well-equipped' house 'with a large garden and a playing field for children'.

Chapter 11

Social Progress, 1890–1940

Not all immigrant families from Eastern Europe achieved success in Manchester. Some, failing to find suitable employment, sought better opportunities, again not always successfully, in other British cities, in South Africa or in the United States. Others remained chained for a lifetime and more to low-paid work and slum-housing. From the late 1880s, however, there were signs that the majority had, to varying extents, 'made good': in better paid and more stable occupations, as independent industrialists, merchants and shopkeepers, as members of the professions or, at the top of the scale, as the owners of substantial mercantile or manufacturing concerns.

Children at the door of a house in Davison Street, Red Bank, c.1920. (Courtesy Manchester Jewish Museum.)

The Rose brothers on cycles, c.1905. Two of the Rose brothers were founders of Great Universal Stores in Manchester, one of the first mail-order businesses in Britain. (Courtesy Manchester Jewish Museum.)

Settlement of Higher Broughton

Such progress made patterns on the ground. In north Manchester the more successful merchants and industrialists of Eastern European origin, including Michael Marks, the prosperous rag dealer Ephraim Sieff (father of Israel Sieff, Michael Marks's son-in-law), and the calico printer Samuel Finburgh, sought mansions in the semi-rural and supposedly healthier Higher Broughton district of Salford. In this very English setting they created cricket, tennis and literary clubs, at which their sons might receive an education in the leisure pursuits,

Group of working-class boys in a street in Strangeways, c.1930. (Courtesy Manchester Jewish Museum.)

manners and etiquette of the English middle classes, but within the safety of an Orthodox Jewish social life in which the Sabbath was observed, the food kosher and all the members Jewish. It was in these refined settings, too, that the children of this Eastern European elite might be expected to find 'suitable' wives among their social peers. There also, in April 1905, they created a temporary place of worship for around 120 Higher Broughton families, in a house in Duncan Street, before opening the Higher Broughton Synagogue in September 1907, a purpose-built and prestigious place of worship on the same site which was to prove, through its social and cultural events, a forcing house of communal and civic leadership.

Members of the synagogue who achieved political fame included Sam Finburgh, Mayor of Salford and the first Manchester Jewish MP for a local constituency (Salford in 1924); Abraham Moss, later Lord

Mayor of Manchester and President of the Jewish Board of Deputies, and Leslie Lever, a Manchester city councillor, Lord Mayor and Labour MP. Its communal leaders included Lawrence Kostoris, a textile exporter and long-time president of the Jewish Home for the Aged, and Isidore Sandler and Samuel Davis, both presidents of the Jewish Representative Council. One of the earliest ministers of the Higher Broughton, the Revd Dr Abraham Cohen, later became president of the Jewish Board of Deputies; another, Rabbi Bernard Casper, went on to become Chief Rabbi of South Africa.

Class at Jews' School, c.1927–28. (Courtesy Manchester Jewish Museum.)

ABOVE LEFT: Mr and Mrs Solomon Laser outside their home in Cheetham Hill. (Courtesy Manchester Jewish Museum.)

Hightown, Crumpsall and Prestwich

By the 1890s the centre of gravity of working-class Jewry was moving northwards from Red Bank and Strangeways towards Hightown, an area of neat terraced property dating from the 1850s and 1860s, when speculative building had converted the rural districts of Cheetham Hill into 'a wilderness of bricks and mortar'. In spite of resistance from at least one native landlord, and references in the local press to 'the Jewish invasion of an English suburb', the renting of houses in Hightown had become the preference of Jewish skilled artisans, shopkeepers, travellers in jewellery and clothing and workshop masters of modest success. By 1895 there were enough Jewish families in Hightown to warrant the renting of a house in Bell Street for use as the first Hightown Synagogue.

*The Sephardi merchant, Isaac Cansino, making a **barmitzvah** present to his son, 1926.*

One of the Eastern European synagogue functionaries (appointed by the Strangeways Synagogue in Harris Street), who occasionally delivered sermons in the Hightown Synagogue, was the father of Louis Golding who, after an education at the Manchester Jews' School, Manchester Grammar School and Queen's College in Oxford, went on to write *Magnolia Street* (1932), the first, and most successful, of a series of novels based on his experience as a Hightown resident. The real Magnolia Street, on which Jews occupied houses on one side of the road and non-Jews on the other, is said to have been Sycamore Street, one of a series of arboreal streets in Hightown. By 1914 there were at least two other Hightown congregations, the New Hightown, in a former Protestant church on Waterloo Road, and the Rydal Mount Synagogue in Elizabeth Street.

Hightown was the staging point from which more socially ambitious working-class Jewish families made their way, in two or three generations, from the immigrant slums of Red Bank, Strangeways and Lower Broughton, and the steadily decaying property of the rest of Cheetham, to the semi-detached property built in the 1920s and 1930s by speculative builders, some of them Jewish, in the suburbs of Crumpsall and Prestwich. Their progress 'up the hill' along Cheetham Hill Road (which, in its northern progress, became Bury Old Road) was marked by new orthodox synagogues within walking distance of their homes. The first was created in 1922 by the conversion of a house, Rosen Hallas, near the junction of Cheetham Hill Road and Leicester Road in Crumpsall. During 1928–29 it was replaced on the same site by the purpose-built Higher Crumpsall Synagogue, which opened officially in September 1929. In 1928 the congregation of the Central Synagogue moved from the corner of Park Street into a new building in Heywood Street, off the upper reaches of Cheetham Hill Road. The synagogue was initially situated in Red Bank in the 1860s as the Chevra Torah and moved in the 1890s into a building on the edge of Red Bank, known popularly as Claff's Shool. In 1935 it became the main component of a purpose-built Art Deco-style synagogue, the Holy Law, designed by the local architect Theodor H. Birks on Bury Old Road, Prestwich. It was destined to become

Louis Golding, the Manchester-born Jewish novelist, 1949. (Courtesy Manchester Jewish Museum.)

Emmanuel and Bella Rebeiro outside their home in Hightown, c.1930. (Courtesy Manchester Jewish Museum.)

the major place of worship for Prestwich Jewry. Other new synagogues for the suburban north were the Heaton Park Hebrew Congregation, founded in a converted house on Middleton Road, Prestwich, in 1937 by the Orthodox insurance broker, Eli Fox, and the Prestwich Hebrew Congregation, still known as 'the Shrubberies' after the house in which it was constructed in 1938.

Meantime, Manchester's 'Cathedral' Synagogue, the Great, had felt the need to adjust to the death of its older members and 'the migration [of a younger generation] to the northern suburbs'. In 1935 and 1936, temporary accommodation was found for 100 of its members in the Crumpsall and Prestwich areas. As it became clear that the shift in the centre of gravity of its membership was irreversible, in 1937 the congregation purchased a large house known as Stenecourt, in Singleton Road, Crumpsall, for use as a place of worship and religious education. During 1938–39 this 'branch synagogue' was extended to hold 200 worshippers (and, finally, a new building was constructed on the site in 1954).

Ward and Mitchells Electrical Goods Shop at the corner of Waterloo Road and Percival Street, Hightown. (Courtesy Manchester Jewish Museum.)

BOTTOM RIGHT: Rose's Smart Toilet Saloon, c.1930.

BOTTOM LEFT: David Angelofsky's shoe-repairing shop in Clarendon Street, All Saints, c.1910.

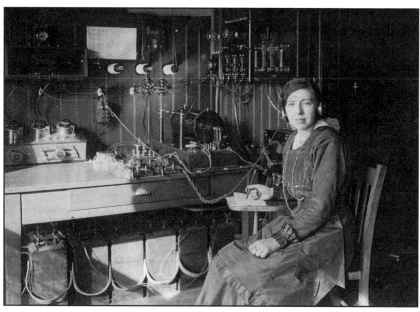

The northwards movement was accelerated in the late 1930s by the slum clearance of Red Bank (1938–39) and during the war by the Blitz, in which several Jewish buildings, including the Reform Synagogue in Park Place and the nurses' home attached to the Jewish hospital, were severely damaged.

Dolly Aaron as a wireless telegrapher in Manchester, 1920.

Fallowfield, Withington and Didsbury

To the south of the city, the relatively well-to-do Jewish families around All Saints, Chorlton-on-Medlock and Victoria Park, who in 1872 had created the first South Manchester Synagogue, moved southwards along the line of Oxford Road, first to the village of Fallowfield, where in August 1913 a new South Manchester Synagogue, conspicuous for its dome and 65ft tower, designed by the local Jewish architect, Joseph Sunlight, was opened on Wilbraham Road, and then towards Withington and Didsbury. Sephardi merchant families had made their home in mansions along and around Palatine Road since the 1890s. They created the Withington Congregation of Spanish and Portuguese Jews first, in 1904, after purchasing Mosley Lodge (for £950),

The mansion in Higher Broughton, 'Woodcliffe,' which was home to the Henriques family.

a house in Mauldeth Road in Withington village and then, in 1927, in grand, purpose-built premises in Queens Road, designed in classical monumental style by the London Jewish architect Delissa Joseph, capable of housing 700 worshippers. The synagogue was founded by speakers of Ladino, the Sephardi equivalent of Yiddish, in their case a mixture of Hebrew and Spanish. Nearby, in Old Landsdowne Road, Arabic-speaking Sephardim (the so-called

Baghdadians), chiefly from Syria and Iraq, dissatisfied with the ritual established at Queens Road by their Ladino-speaking co-religionists, built the small but handsome Sha'are Sedek Synagogue in 1925. The two Sephardi synagogues, which continued to coexist, each with its own rabbi, until their amalgamation in 1997, were distinguished religiously only by minor ritual variations. It has been estimated that, of the 200 Sephardi households in Manchester by 1930, 175 were living in south Manchester.

Broughton High School, a private school in Higher Broughton attended by many of the children of wealthier Jewish families, c.1920. (Courtesy Manchester Jewish Museum.)

The opulent world of this Sephardi cottonocracy of south Manchester at its formative stage is vividly brought to life in the autobiography of the Nobel prize-winning novelist, Elias Canetti, *The Tongue Set Free*. As a child, Canetti lived with his family in Withington during 1911–13.

Machzikei Hadass

Social progress, whether northwards or into the southern suburbs, was also part of a process of acculturation, as suburbanising Jewish families modelled their domestic and social lives on those of the English middle class. The degree to which, in these new settings, they adhered to Jewish custom varied widely. The many who drifted away from Jewish observance incurred the displeasure of the orthodox and, particularly, of those strictly observant of Jewish custom. These included a group of businessmen in the textile trade, mainly fent dealers, who had arrived in Manchester at the turn of the 19th century, chiefly from Brody in Galicia, and in the summer of 1925 founded the Machzikei Hadass Society to signal the extent of their opposition to the erosion of religious orthodoxy and, as a religious beacon, to alert the community as a whole to the importance of 'authentic Judaism'. At first no more than a tiny pressure group drawn from, and meeting in, the Polish Synagogue

The Higher Broughton Synagogue in Duncan Street. (Courtesy Manchester Jewish Museum.)

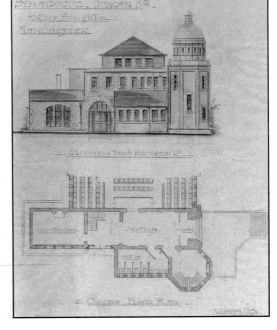

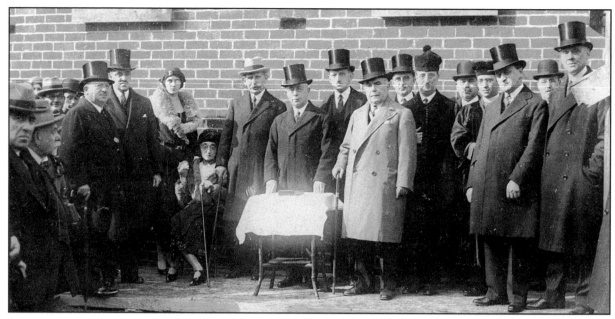

The Committee of the Higher Broughton Synagogue c.1920. (Courtesy Manchester Jewish Museum.)

in Strangeways, they evolved in time into the nucleus of a strictly observant kehillah [society] in the Higher Broughton and Broughton Park areas of Salford and the Sedgley Park district of Prestwich.

Wedding photograph of Annie Glickman and Isaac Bursk outside Higher Broughton Town Hall, 1921. (Courtesy Manchester Jewish Museum.)

Political allegiance

Social progress also brought changes in the political allegiance of the Jewish people who enjoyed it. Social dispersal brought with it political diversity. Until the 1890s most Jewish people were attached to Liberalism, largely on the grounds that it was the Liberal Party that had fought most strongly for Jewish emancipation. By the mid-1890s, however, political allegiance was increasingly determined more by class than by ethnicity.

There is evidence that some, at least, of the more successful entrepreneurs of Eastern European origin, as well as some of the longer-established merchants of German origin, were turning to the political right. This included, for example, Isidore Frankenburg, a man of Russo-Polish origin, who by the early

1890s had created the Greengate and Irwell Rubber Company for the manufacture of rubber, leather and waterproof goods. In 1896 Frankenburg was elected in the Conservative interest to represent Grosvenor Ward on Salford City Council and subsequently served for three

Jewish Garden Party in Higher Broughton c.1911. (Courtesy Manchester Jewish Museum.)

years as Mayor of the city. Other early Conservatives were the Russian-born Nathan Hope, whose Anchor Cap Works was in Derby Street, Cheetham; the Galician fent dealer, Bernard Kostoris; the waterproof garment manufacturer, Jacob Weinberg, and the textile dealer and calico printer, Samuel Finburgh. Of older Jewish families, the Henriques and the Samsons were pillars of the Manchester Conservative Party.

The election campaign of Winston Churchill, who fought the North West Manchester constituency as a Liberal in 1905, attracted, in his support, Jewish Liberals under Nathan Laski and, in opposition, Jewish Conservatives mobilised by the Sephardi cotton merchant, David Garson. Churchill's victory in the Manchester constituency with the largest Jewish population suggests that, at that date, Liberalism had maintained its hold on the Jewish population. His defeat, when he stood for a second (and last) time for North West Manchester in 1908, may indicate the beginning of a more general break-up of the love affair between

Members of the Cassel family, 1910. Adolf Cassel was a builder who, among many other buildings, created the Higher Broughton Assembly Rooms. (Courtesy Manchester Jewish Museum.)

Jews and Liberalism. After 1905 an increasing number of working-class Jews gave their support to the new Labour party.

Other working-class members of the younger Jewish generation were attracted to the more radical politics of the left. Some were from families which had leaned to the left even before their departure from Russia. Others had been drawn leftwards by their experiences in Manchester.

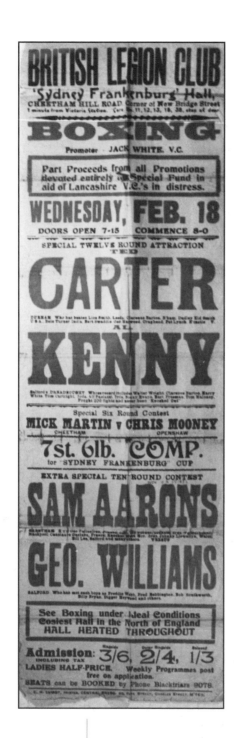

Boy at entrance of Bellott Street Park, a favoured resort of Jewish families in Cheetham, 1927. (Courtesy Manchester Jewish Museum.)

The Strovitch family of Manchester with the family car, a sure sign of social progress, in the 1930s. (Courtesy Manchester Jewish Museum.)

Poster advertising the appearance of the Jewish boxer, Sam Aarons. (Courtesy Manchester Jewish Museum.)

Jewish Boy Scouts, 1928. (Courtesy Manchester Jewish Museum.)

Manchester Jewish family on holiday in Southport, the favoured seaside resort of Manchester Jewish families, in 1910. Some of the wealthier Manchester Jewish businessmen had homes in Southport and commuted daily by train. (Courtesy Manchester Jewish Museum.)

A typical street in Hightown. (Courtesy Manchester Jewish Museum.)

Coronation Party,
Thirlmere Street,
Hightown, 1953.
(Courtesy Manchester
Jewish Museum.)

While immigrant parents had felt compelled to accept, without undue complaint, life in the slums and work in the sweat shops as the price of their safety in Britain, many of their children found such circumstances unacceptable. One response was a flight to the suburbs just as soon as this became financially possible. Other children, a minority, found an explanation for such conditions in Marxism. Leading the way in this direction were three of the four sons of the Lithuanian immigrant, Solomon Abrahamson (later Ainley), a Socialist who had arrived in Manchester during the 1880s to become a skilled worker in the manufacture of umbrellas and walking sticks, while his Latvian-born wife ran a tiny newspaper shop in Ancoats. Abrahamson celebrated his Socialism by naming his first son William Morris. Moving to Hightown and at the same time returning to his religious roots, the two sons who followed were given the traditional Jewish names David and Benjamin. Following his conversion to Zionism, his fourth son became Theodore Herzl. In their own later reality, William Morris (anglicised to Maurice) became the family Zionist, while David, Benjamin and Theodore ('Teddy') were all attracted to the left.

Ben Ainley became one of a group of young people, all children of immigrants of Eastern European origin, most of them unemployed, who in 1919 began to meet informally at the Ainley home to debate political issues. Calling themselves 'The Pioneers', by 1921 they had adopted a Marxist ideology to become founder members of the Cheetham branch of the Young Communist League (YCL), a branch in which Jewish members (rising to 200) always formed a majority. They included the young engineer Benny Rothman, who in 1932 led the Kinder Scout Mass Trespass, the pioneering event in the struggle to gain access to the countryside. Of the five 'trespassers' who tangled

Lily Gerber outside her house in Chestnut Street, Hightown, 1934. (Courtesy Manchester Jewish Museum.)

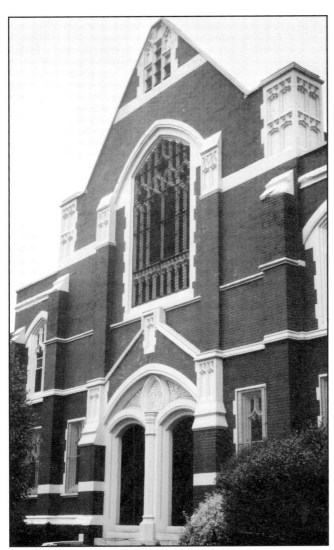

The Central and North Manchester Synagogue, Leicester Road, Crumpsall, 1959. (Courtesy Manchester Jewish Museum.)

Programme for Gypsy Love performed by the Manchester Jewish Amateur Operatic Society, 1928. (Courtesy Manchester Jewish Museum.)

Julie Emmanuel with the Manchester Maccabi Minstrels, 1950s. (Courtesy Manchester Jewish Museum.)

Members of the cast of Cinderelly, *a haimisher pantomime written and directed by Julie Emmanuel, 1948. (Courtesy Manchester Jewish Museum.)*

Scene from a play performed by the Manchester Great Synagogue Dramatic Society. (Courtesy Manchester Jewish Museum.)

The South Manchester Synagogue in Wilbraham Road, designed by the Manchester Jewish architect, Joseph Sunlight, and opened in 1913. (Courtesy Manchester Jewish Museum.)

Laying of the foundation stone of the South Manchester Synagogue, 1913. (Courtesy Manchester Jewish Museum.)

Joseph Hakim standing with Torah Scroll outside the first Sephardi Synagogue in south Manchester, in Mauldeth Road, c.1920. (Courtesy Manchester Jewish Museum.)

The children of Joseph and Reina Hakim, Sephardi residents of Didsbury, c.1920. (Courtesy Manchester Jewish Museum.)

Interior of the Withington Congregation of Spanish and Portuguese Jews. (Courtesy Mike Poloway.)

The Withington Congregation of Spanish and Portuguese Jews. (Courtesy Mike Poloway.)

Withington Jewish Girl Guides, 1930s. (Courtesy Manchester Jewish Museum.)

with police and gamekeepers to earn short terms of imprisonment with hard labour, two – Rothman and the garment maker and trade unionist Yudel ('Juddy') Clyne – were Jewish. After 1933 these same YCLers, including the waterproof garment worker Martin Bobker, played a leading role in the Trade Union movement and in orchestrating militant opposition to Oswald Mosley's British Union of Fascists, who in 1934 had set up their northern headquarters at 17 Northumberland Street, Higher Broughton, close to the Jewish Quarter. After 1936 some, as convinced anti-fascists, left Manchester through the agency of the full-time organiser of the regional branch of the Communist Party, Mick Jenkins, himself Jewish, to fight with the British Battalion of the International Brigade in the Spanish Civil War. These included the young tailor Benny Goodman, the waterproof garment maker Maurice Levine, and the barber Bert Maisky, who died at the Battle of Jarama in 1937. Those who returned, with their base at the YCL's Challenge Club in Hightown, continued their anti-fascist activities in Manchester, some to the point of imprisonment, until in 1937 Mosley was persuaded to close his northern headquarters. With some degree of poetic justice, the building the fascists had used was then purchased in 1938 by the Jewish businessman, A.J. Pfeffer, for use as the synagogal base of the Jewish Orthodox pressure group Machzikei Hadass.

The Manchester community of today includes a close-knit group of Jewish families, among them the Ainleys and the Clynes, bonded by their common experience of YCL, the Communist Party of Great Britain and the anti-fascism of the 1930s. One of them was the late Frank Allaun, the son of a Jewish language teacher, who in the 1930s was manager of Collet's [radical] bookshop and the Manchester agent of the Left Book Club. He was later a member of the Communist Party, a radical Labour MP for Salford East and an active vice-president of the Campaign for Nuclear Disarmament. Members of the group were among the founders, and remain the supporters, of what is now the Working-Class Movement Library in Salford.

Chapter 12

Manchester Jewry in the 1930s

By 1933 the number of identifying Jews in Manchester had stabilised at around 35,000. The vast majority belonged to the second or third generation of families of Eastern European origin. Only a few of the Jewish families whose early 19th-century origins lay in Germany and Holland now remained. Many had moved to London, some had returned to their home countries, particularly in the face of the fierce anti-German feeling generated by World War One. Others, including the descendants of the Jewish architect Edward Salomon, had left Judaism for some form of Christianity, married out or, for other reasons, severed all ties with the community. Of course, like any other society, Manchester Jewry had its 'comers and goers'. Among the former were immigrants from other communities of British Jewry, some of whom married into Manchester Jewish families, while others came as students to Manchester University, only to remain in the city after

Party at the Higher Broughton Assembly Rooms, c.1930. (Courtesy Manchester Jewish Museum.)

Offices of the Jewish
Chronicle *and the*
Manchester Jewish
Gazette. *c.1940.*
*(Courtesy Manchester
Central Library.)*

*A Christmas party for
machinists from Kendal
and Jacob's raincoat
factory in Derby Street,
c.1930. (Courtesy
Manchester Jewish
Museum.)*

graduation. The search for work, particularly in the professions, brought other Jews, old and young, into the community with their families. Among the 'goers' were those tempted by the continuing attraction of the United States and those who left for the British dominions, for other parts of provincial Jewry or for London, with its more richly diverse Jewish life. Between the wars, while its total Jewish population varied very little, the community was always, in these ways, in a state of flux.

For Jewish people, the 1930s were years of sharp contrasts. In Europe the Nazis assumed power in Germany in 1933 to commence their 'war against the Jews'. In Manchester, the Jewish garment and furniture industries, as well as Jewish overseas traders, were hard hit by the repercussions of the slump in world trade which began in 1929. Depression undermined the prosperity of many Sephardi merchants still engaged in the textile trade. Throughout the 1930s, Jewish manual workers fought hard to retain their hard-earned rates of pay and working conditions. At the same time, more fortunate Jewish families were enabled by accessible mortgages and speculative building to move in increasing numbers into the attractive northern suburbs of Crumpsall and Prestwich, or southwards towards the equally alluring Cheadle. One observer saw the old Jewish Quarter on Cheetham Hill as being increasingly 'denuded' of Jewish residents and certainly, by the outbreak of World War Two, a 'new Jewish Quarter' had decisively taken shape across its northern boundary.

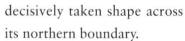

For many younger Jews, this was the 'jazz age': a time of dance bands (some with Jewish leaders), cinemas (some under Jewish ownership), new forms of leisure and mildly hedonistic partying. In October 1932 a group of Jewish businessmen founded Whitefield Golf Club,

Manchester's first Jewish golf club, largely, it is said, to counter the exclusion of Jews from existing clubs. The builder Adolf Cassel, angered that his daughters had been refused entry to a Prestwich tennis club, founded the Waterpark Club as a centre of leisure (and tennis) for the Jewish young. For the politicised, it was equally a time for anti-fascist activity on the Manchester streets and for a militant struggle in

Staff dance at Hollstein and Portnoy's garment factory in Cheetham, 1930s. (Courtesy Manchester Jewish Museum.)

Manchester factories (such as long strikes in the waterproof industry during 1934–35 and 1938–39). For others still, it was a time, in response to these 'secular' developments, for a return to more traditional Orthodox observance. There was also increasingly intense Zionist activity as the spread of Nazism and endemic anti-Semitism suggested the precariousness of Jewish life in the Diaspora.

It was also the beginning of an era of refugees, some of whom chose Manchester as their haven of safety. Between 1933 and 1940, between six and eight thousand Jews arrived in Manchester from Germany and from the countries overtaken by German expansion: Austria, Czechoslovakia and Poland. Mounting discrimination in the Arab world following the creation of the Jewish State

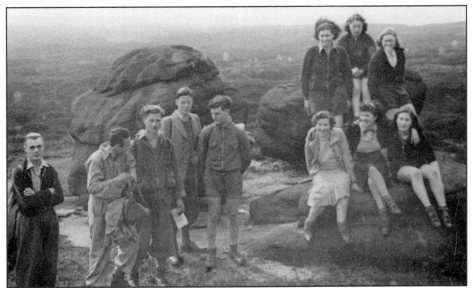

Jewish members of the Young Communist League on a ramble in the Cheshire countryside, 1930s. (Courtesy Manchester Jewish Museum.)

Edward Isaacs, the blind Jewish pianist and organiser of the popular Tuesday Lunchtime Concerts in Manchester throughout the 1930s, pictured in 1945. (Courtesy Manchester Jewish Museum.)

A group of tenants outside the Mad Hatters Castle in Whalley Range with their landlady, Martha Butt. (Copyright Manchester Central Library.)

in 1948 brought Iranian, Iraqi and Egyptian Jews to the city, although in much smaller numbers. The Prague Spring of 1956 provided a new stimulus for the migration of Czech Jews, a few of whom reached Manchester. Finally, also in 1956, the Russian invasion of Hungary brought Hungarian Jewish families to Manchester, as they escaped the repression of the Communist regime.

Refugees from Nazism

With the advent of Hitler as Chancellor of Germany in 1933 and the consolidation of his Nazi regime, the Nazi Government began its increasingly vicious attack upon its Jewish citizens. Hitler's rabid anti-Semitism was converted by his minions into discriminatory legislation which gradually restricted the rights of all those judged by the Nazis to be 'Jewish': not only practising Jews but, according to the infamous Nuremberg Laws of 1936, all those with at least one Jewish grandparent, even those who had long abandoned their links with Judaism. The victims of what was essentially part of a racial attack on non-Aryans, including converts to Christianity, now defined in Nazi ideology as non-Aryan Christians. Between 1933 and 1939 Jewish rights were progressively restricted, Jewish property seized, Jewish people assaulted and humiliated, their status as citizens removed. The Nazi objective in these years had not extended to genocide: the aim was first the marginalisation and then the enforced emigration of the 500,000 Jews who had earlier played such a prominent role in German economic, political and cultural life.

The world outside Germany was not freely open to Jewish resettlement. Fear of competition from German immigrants at a time of high unemployment, combined with traditional anti-Semitic prejudice, meant that the response to Jewish refugees in the United States and throughout Europe was, at best, timid and circumspect. No country, and this included Britain, was prepared to launch a large-scale rescue operation. In Britain the restrictions faced by all 'alien immigrants' were applied equally to German Jews.

The right of entry other than as visitors was limited to those who could offer proof, either in the form of the offer of work or the support of a British guarantor, that they would not become dependent on state funds. Only those forms of employment, for which no British candidates were available, were open to German immigrants. Britain did not see herself as a country of immigration. Even those who found guarantors, permitted jobs or traineeships were expected to move on in due course to other countries or emigrate to one such country. Settlement in Palestine, then a British mandate, was severely limited by Britain's unwillingness to antagonise its Arab population.

While the emigration of German-Jewish families began on a small scale in 1933, at first chiefly to countries neighbouring Germany, most German Jews were slow to move. Many believed that the Nazi regime was a temporary aberration which would be followed in due course by a return to democracy. Others believed that, once secure in their hold on power, the Nazis would temper or abandon their anti-Semitic programme. There was a natural reluctance among German Jews to uproot their families from the nation they still regarded as their home. Others were put off (or held off) by the barriers to immigration posted in the countries of the West. The disinclination to move ended only when the atrocities which followed the Anschluss (Austria's 'reunion' with Germany) of March 1938, the horrors of Kristallnacht (the night of 9–10 November 1938) and the rape of Czechoslovakia in March 1939 convinced most Jewish Germans of the permanence of the Nazi regime and its anti-Semitic programme. In the case of Britain, perhaps 10,000 German-Jewish refugees entered the country before 1938, some subsequently returning hopefully to Germany. A further 60,000 arrived from Germany, Austria, Czechoslovakia and Poland during 1938–39.

Advert for the firm of the Jewish bookmaker, Gus Demmy. (Courtesy Manchester Jewish Museum.)

Gus Demmy on a racecourse. (Courtesy Manchester Jewish Museum.)

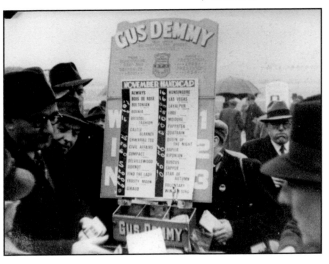

Jewish group with coach outside Sam's barber shop, 1929, preparing to leave for Blackpool. (Courtesy Manchester Jewish Museum.)

Eddie Cantor playing as an honorary member of Whitefield Golf Club, July 1938. (Courtesy Manchester Jewish Museum.)

In the case of Manchester, perhaps 500 German refugees had reached the city by March 1938, chiefly those expelled from the German professions, Jewish industrialists whose firms had been taken over or placed at risk, young women employed as domestic servants (one of the few occupations open to aliens) and young trainees who were expected to depart once their training was complete. A further 6–7,000 refugees, now also from Austria and Czechoslovakia, arrived after the Anschluss and the German occupation of the Czech provinces of Bohemia and Moravia in March 1939. Statistics are not available to break down these figures with precision in terms of nationality. Such evidence that has survived suggests a body of Czech refugees not over 400 individuals, very few Poles and the rest perhaps evenly balanced between Austrians and Germans. At least 85 per cent of all refugees were Jewish. The rest was made up of 'politicals' (Socialist, Communist, Liberal and pacifist) persecuted as opponents of the Nazi regime. The total includes 1,000 of the 10,000 children allowed into Britain, by a rare but important concession, on Kindertransports from Berlin, Vienna, Prague and Warsaw.

Poster advertising a performance of the Jewish Amateur Minstrels at Ancoats Lads' Club. (Courtesy Manchester Jewish Museum.)

Hyman Lurie, a table tennis player of national note and former member of the Grove House Lads' Club, 1933. (Courtesy Manchester Jewish Museum.)

The Reception of Refugees

Their reception in Manchester was mixed, particularly before 1938. Naturally sympathetic to their oppressed co-religionists, the Jewish community responded at once with appeals for funds to support the Central British Fund (CBF), created in 1933 by the British Jewish elite to ease the sufferings of German Jewry and lend support to refugees. Led by Nathan Laski, however, the Manchester Jewish Representative Council, remembering the furore which had accompanied the earlier 'alien invasion', was at first reluctant to take any measure which might be seen to encourage alien settlement in Manchester. Most council members shared Laski's view that the most appropriate destination for Jewish refugees was Palestine, a view also endorsed by the CBF and by

Jewish Manchester City supporters travelling to watch the Blues play Grimsby in 1936. (Courtesy Manchester Jewish Museum.)

Fundraising event by the Great Synagogue Literary and Social Society.

THE EVENT OF THE SEASON

in aid of the

'Morris Laski' Memorial Orphan Fund
of the Manchester Jewish Orphan Aid Society

The
GREAT SYNAGOGUE LITERARY AND SOCIAL SOCIETY
DRAMATIC SECTION
(Winners for the 3rd time of the Jewish Drama Festival Shield)
WILL PRESENT
For the First Time on any Stage
A Great New Modern Play in Three Acts.

"Beneath the Skin"

BY EMMANUEL LEVY the well-known Manchester Artist
at the **LESSER FREE TRADE HALL**, Peter Street,
on Monday. Tuesday, Wednesday, Thursday and Saturday,
December 11th, 12th, 13th, 14th and 16th.

Curtain rises promptly at 7·30 p.m.   :   :   Prices 1/- to **5/-**

Seats may be booked in advance at
14. BLACKFRIARS STREET, DEANSGATE
(Hon. Organiser, Mr. L. Kay) - - Phone BLA 4444.
Tickets also obtainable at the Offices of the
"JEWISH GAZETTE," 97, Cheetham Hill Rd.
and on Sunday Morning at Frankenburg House, 184 Cheetham Hill Rd

'PATRONS' for a fee of 1 Guinea are entitled to Four Special Seats
'SUBSCRIBERS' for Ten Shillings, to Two

A GOOD SHOW for a GOOD CAUSE

the local branch of the Jewish National Fund. At most, Laski was prepared to support an effort led by the local jeweller, Isidore Apfelbaum, to find places as temporary trainees for young refugees. Independently of the council, the influential Manchester Ladies Lodge of the Order B'nai Brith created a Hospitality Committee which gave support, social and financial, to young refugee women arriving as domestic servants. At first, the Manchester Yeshiva offered studentships to no more than a handful of Orthodox refugees. Outside the Jewish community, between 1933 and 1938, the University of Manchester offered temporary fellowships to 20 academics, most of them Jewish, expelled from universities in Germany and Austria, while the Manchester Society of Friends (the Quakers) gave a degree of aid to 10 or 12 families of fleeing German pacifists. During 1938 a group of Liberal internationalists, inspired by the Quakers, laid the basis of the Manchester International Club in premises in George Street, in central Manchester, which opened in the following year (and which are now part of Manchester's City Art Gallery). In its conception, although intended for foreign students, it attracted many refugees to its social and cultural events and became, in fact, a place at which refugees typically met to exchange information and ideas and to form friendships and relationships, some of which lasted for their lifetimes.

The local mood changed decisively in the face of the escalating arrival of refugees after the Anschluss and Kristallnacht. In November 1938 formal refugee committees were set up by the Jewish community and by the Quakers. Their negotiated agreement was that while the Jewish Refugees Committee aided the arrival and settlement of those defined as 'practising Jews', the Quaker Refugee Committee of Manchester and District dealt with non-Jews and with those described as non-practising Jews and non-Aryan Christians. In fact, some 40 per cent of refugees helped by the Quakers were of Jewish origin, including some who were practising. Until the outbreak of war, the work of both committees – with no government aid and run entirely by unpaid volunteers – centred on easing the emigration and settlement of refugees. Soon after the outbreak of war, the British Government, recognising that the funds of most voluntary organisations had now been used up, agreed to subsidise the refugee committees, including the two in Manchester, in their work of accommodating and maintaining refugees who had settled in Manchester. While still dependent to an extent on local funds and, even more, on local volunteers, the Jewish and Quaker committees became, in fact, state-subsidised welfare agencies dealing with the onerous material, advisory and spiritual support of refugees.

Morris Levine of Manchester (second from left) with fellow members of the International Brigade in Spain. (Courtesy Manchester Jewish Museum.)

Between 1938 and 1945 the two committees set up, between them, eight refugee hostels in Manchester and found accommodation for other refugees with private families or in lodging houses like 'the Mad Hatters Castle' in Whalley Range, the visitors' book of which, full of German and Austrian refugees, has recently found its way into the archives of Manchester Central

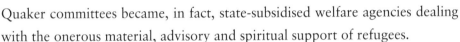

Squad of fire guards stationed at the factory of David Matz, who manufactured the naptha solution used by Jewish waterproofers, c.1940. (Courtesy Manchester Jewish Museum.)

Jewish members of the Land Army. (Courtesy Manchester Jewish Museum.)

Display stand for waterproof garments and rainwear produced at the Cohen and Wilks factory in Derby Street, Cheetham. (Courtesy Manchester Jewish Museum.)

Library. In 1939 the two refugee committees also cooperated in the establishment of a regional branch of the Refugee Children's Movement (RCM), which took responsibility for Kindertransport children housed with families in Manchester, Salford, Lancashire and the Lake District. The RCM for what was officially 'Region 10' organised the visiting of children in foster homes to ensure that they were being properly cared for, to offer them support and advice and, in the case of Jewish children, to see that due attention was being paid to their religious needs. During 1939–40, 20 Kindertransport girls were housed at Harris House in Southport, a private house loaned to the Southport branch of the Refugee Children's Movement. The diary of their first year in Britain is now among the treasured items in the storeroom of the Manchester Jewish Museum.

In July 1939 the Manchester Women's Lodge of the Order B'nai Brith opened a hostel in Waterloo Road, Cheetham, for children from Yavne School, a Jewish secondary school in Cologne. The headmaster of the school, Dr Menachem Erich Klibansky, aware of Nazi intentions, had decided in late 1938 to evacuate his school children class by class to Britain, where he hoped that in due course the whole school would be reconstituted. The first two classes arrived in January 1939 in London. A third class was put up in a hostel in Liverpool in the following May. Finally, in mid-July, 18 girls from the school were accommodated at the Waterloo Road hostel, an ageing mansion donated to B'nai Brith by the clothier and property developer Myer Kersh. They remained at what became Myer Kersh House, and found jobs in Manchester or places in Manchester schools, until the hostel closed in 1945. Sadly, Dr Klibansky's scheme did not come to fruition. Trapped in Cologne by the

Group of workers on a Glassberg's rainwear factory outing. (Courtesy Manchester Jewish Museum.)

Louis Berkowitz outside his hardware shop in Waterloo Road, c.1930. (Courtesy Manchester Jewish Museum.)

Badge worn by children on the Kindertransports during their journey to Britain, 1938–39.

Members of the Black and Marks families in the yard of 128 Broughton Lane, Strangeways, 1930s. (Courtesy Manchester Jewish Museum.)

Handbill produced by the Manchester Child Refugees Committee, appealing for contributions towards a hostel for 600 boys, 1939. (Courtesy Manchester Jewish Museum.)

I HAVE YOUTH VIGOUR AND HEALTH

yet they say no one wants me.

HELP ME TO KEEP MY FAITH THAT YOU WILL RESCUE ME FROM A HOPELESS FUTURE

600 REFUGEE BOYS

PLEAD FOR A START IN LIFE

This Appeal is on behalf of the 14 year to 17 year old German Refugee Boys (Jewish and non-Aryan Christian), whose sufferings have been generally recognised, but for whom no offers of hospitality have been received.

We can give these boys training in Technical Schools or as Apprentices, to fit them to go forth to other lands, equipped to make their own way in the world, but homes must be found for them—and found quickly.

Will You Help us to open a Hostel in our Area for some of these Boys?

Will **You**, as an individual, contribute as much as you can spare?

or

Will **You** and **Your Friends** form Yourselves into a Refugee Youth Club and, by regular collections, each week, make yourselves responsible for the maintenance—and happiness—of **I Boy** out of the 600?

Four of the many ways by which different groups of people could form Refugee Youth Clubs :—

15 Business and Professional People each giving I/- per week will keep I boy for I week
30 Housewives ... ... 6d. .. .. ..
60 Students ... ... 3d. .. .. ..
180 School Children... ... . Id. .. .. ..

Weekly Collecting Cards, for those who will help in this way, will be supplied on request.

CAN YOU IGNORE THIS CRY FOR HELP?

It might be **YOUR SON — YOUR BROTHER — YOUR NEPHEW — YOUR FRIEND**

All Contributions should be sent to
The Manchester Child Refugee Committee, 3, Spring Gardens, Manchester 2.

In Association with
The German Jewish Aid Committee, The Society of Friends Refugee Committee, Manchester, Salford & District Council of Christian Congregations.

The Yavne School in Cologne, whose pupils the headmaster sought to save by sending them, class by class, to Britain as refugees. Eighteen came to Manchester in 1939 under the auspices of the Manchester Ladies Lodge of the Order B'nai Brith, which acquired a mansion in Waterloo Road, named Myer Kersh House after its donor, for their accommodation and support.

German Passport of Yolan Simon, a refugee who arrived in Manchester in 1939. (Courtesy Manchester Jewish Museum.)

The garment factory in Chemnitz of which Oscar Einstein was a director before his departure for Manchester as a refugee. The factory was taken over by a nominee of the Nazi Government.

The mansion on the left of this picture was donated by Myer Kersh to the Manchester Ladies Lodge of the Order B'nai Brith. Its management was shared by the Lodge and the Manchester Jewish Refugees Committee. (Copyright Manchester Central Library.)

Young refugees at Myer Kersh House, with their houseparents, c.1941.

Three refugee girls at Myer Kersh House, c.1941.

outbreak of war, he and his family, with the remaining children from his school, were deported to Minsk, where all were murdered by SS firing squads.

In May 1940, as the German invading army approached Amsterdam, a Christian woman and wife of an Amsterdam banker, Mrs Wijsmuller-Meijer, organised the escape on a coal steamer of over 100 Jews, including 70 children from Germany and Austria, then housed in the city orphanage. In spite of attacks from German planes, the group landed at Liverpool. The children, known thereafter as 'the Dutch Orphans', were subsequently moved on to Wigan and finally to Manchester, where they were housed in two hostels in Heaton Road, Withington, financed at first by the city and later taken over by the Jewish Refugees Committee.

In the face of the increasing oppression of European Jewry, and with Jewish settlement in Palestine increasingly limited by British Government decree, Nathan Laski, and the Representative Council of which he was still president, underwent a change of heart, now encouraging refugee settlement in Manchester and seeking only to coordinate and control it. Other local Jewish organisations rallied independently behind refugee support. The Jewish community in Stockport created a hostel for trainees, for whom it found local

Picnic of refugee boys from the Zionist Hachsharah at Thornham Fold Farm.

work placements. The Jewish Home for the Aged acquired a new house, formerly a rectory, for elderly Jewish refugees who had gained entry through its guarantees of support. The Manchester Yeshiva, in spite of its small size and limited resources, heroically, and risking the wrath of Nathan Laski, sponsored the arrival and maintenance of around 55 refugee students, over half of them from Bratislava. The Yeshiva's Director, Rabbi Moshe Segal, and his management committee effectively challenged Laski's view that the Yeshiva lacked the resources to support so many refugees and the facilities for training them for life and work in Manchester. Among the refugee students from Czechoslovakia was Gabriel Brodie, later to become the highly respected minister of the Great Synagogue.

The religious Zionist organisation Bachad, led by the German refugee Arieh Handler, set up a committee in Manchester which acquired land at Middleton in 1939 – Thornham Fold Farm – for the agricultural and political training of young Zionist refugees for life in Palestine. Thornham Fold, a down-at-heel dairy farm, was one of the two *hachsharoth* (Zionist training centres) set up in the Manchester region during the war years. The other was Kibbutz Hakorim (the 'Miners Kibbutz') set up in Stalybridge in 1943 by the Socialist

Zionist youth movement, Hashomer Hatzair, for the training of young Zionists as 'Bevin Boys' in a local coal mine. Some 20 young Zionists, about half of them refugees, lived in a house organised as a commune with the men

Rabbi Dr Alexander Altmann, the German refugee rabbi who came to Manchester in 1938 as Communal Rabbi.

working in the mine and the women taking other work in the town. Bachad was also important as a stimulus to Jewish orthodoxy in Manchester: its refugee members set up an early local branch of what became the important Zionist youth movement, B'nei Akiva.

In 1934 the Machzikei Hadass Society appointed Dr David Feldmann, a refugee from Leipzig, as its rabbi, a move which did much to expand its membership and to strengthen its influence in the community as a whole. By 1938 the society had its own synagogue (named Yesode Hatorah, 'Foundations of the Torah'), religious school and community centre in a building at 17 Northumberland Street, Higher Broughton, purchased for it by the Orthodox businessman of Polish origin, Abraham Jacob Pfeffer. Another refugee rabbi was Dr Alexander Altmann, the Berliner who, in December 1938, was appointed Manchester's Communal Rabbi

Hildegard Rujder and her father in Berlin prior to their coming to Manchester as refugees.

to bring a degree of cohesion to Manchester's Orthodox synagogues and to enhance Manchester's reputation for Orthodox observance and Jewish learning. Altmann remained in Manchester as Communal Rabbi and head of the Beth Din until his appointment in 1959 to a post in the Department of Philosophy at Brandeis University in the United States. Among his major achievements was the setting up of the Manchester and Salford Institute of Higher Jewish Education in November 1941 which, long after his departure, formed the basis of the present Centre for Postgraduate Hebrew Studies at Yarnton Manor in Oxfordshire. In fostering a higher education in Jewish

Bernard Klein as a boy in Berlin at the time of his barmitzvah. He came to Britain as a refugee in 1939. He joined the Pioneer Corps and, after his discharge on medical grounds, managed a scrap metal business owned by another refugee in Rochdale.

Bernard Klein in the Alien Company of the Pioneer Corps, the only part of the British army which refugees were at first allowed to join. Later in the war many moved on to combat units.

Ruth Schneier with her father and mother in Vienna before her arrival in Manchester as an unaccompanied refugee in January 1939. Both her parents were murdered during the Holocaust.

history and Judaism, Altmann saw himself as offering some compensation for the centres of Jewish learning being devastated by Nazi rule in Eastern Europe.

An unusual development was the creation near Manchester of a community made up substantially of refugees. The drawing together of a group of domestic servants, trainees and other refugees living in and around Wilmslow in Cheshire inspired the Manchester Jewish pacifist, Lionel Cowan, to create the 'Wilmslow Jewish Community' in 1942, which organised its own services and which achieved official recognition from the Chief Rabbi and from the Manchester Jewish Representative Council. As the refugees dispersed from Wilmslow in the post-war years, the new community first amalgamated with the Jewish community in Macclesfield and finally dissolved. More typical was for refugees attached to industries in south Lancashire and Derbyshire – in Glossop and Eccles, for example – to make the journey on the Sabbath to the Manchester Reform Synagogue.

Outside the Jewish and Quaker communities, other altruistic bodies and individuals also gave a measure of support to refugees. During 1939–40 the Manchester Rotary Club established and ran a hostel in north Manchester for refugee trainees in a house donated by the Jewish businessman Lawrence Kostoris. Until the outbreak of war, the University of Manchester continued to award fellowships to displaced scholars from Czechoslovakia, Italy and fascist Spain, as well as Germany and Austria. It also opened its doors to a limited number of refugee students, some of them supported by the Manchester branch of the International Student Service. The Catholic Church took a number of Kindertransport children, some of them of Jewish origin, into its convents and orphanages. Anglican and Non-conformist Christians, although they set up strong national agencies for refugee support in Manchester, tended to work through the Friends Refugee Committee.

In Manchester the refugees also helped themselves, some with the support of the Jewish Refugees Committee, others on their own initiative. With the help of prominent Manchester Liberals, German, Austrian and Czech refugees set up national organisations which had Jewish members. Of these, the largest, the most important and the most attractive to Jewish refugees was the Free German League of Culture, designed, like the other 'national' bodies, to sustain refugees' interest in the pre-Nazi culture of their homeland. A clandestine Manchester branch of the German Communist Party established three hostels in the Manchester area, in Sale, Salford and Victoria Park, and created a propaganda apparatus which attracted some

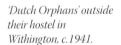

'Dutch Orphans' with their hostel staff, c.1942.

Ruth Schneier's passport, January 1939.

'Dutch Orphans' outside their hostel in Withington, c.1941.

Staff at the hostel in Withington with Rae Barash, third from the left, chair of the Manchester Jewish Refugees Committee.

Jewish support to the party. At the end of the war, it was these 'politicals' who were the most likely to return to their home countries, drawn by nostalgia for a lost way of life or, in the case of Communists, by a desire to participate in the creation of what might then have seemed like utopian left-wing regimes. A large but unknown number of Jewish refugees, perhaps the majority, disillusioned by the activities of their Nazi co-nationals and their allies, opted to remain in Britain or to move on to the United States.

In 1947 Rae Barash, knowing that many of the elderly refugees remaining in Manchester were isolated and distressed, suggested the establishment of a 'home for lonely, infirm and elderly refugees who had been victims of Nazi persecution'. With the help of the Manchester branch of the Association of Jewish Refugees and of refugee industrialists with firms around Manchester, her object was met by the establishment in 1948 in a house in Didsbury of the Morris Feinmann Home, named after her predecessor as chairman of the Jewish Refugees Committee. Translated in 1959 to larger premises in Spath Road, Didsbury, periodically extended, and later opened to all the Jewish elderly, it remains a major element of Jewish communal welfare.

Group of young Refugees on a ramble in the countryside around Manchester. The young man in the foreground is Werner Lachs, now chairman of the Manchester branch of the Association of Jewish Refugees.

Jetzt kommt Chorlton von der Näh'

Bambel guckt zum Fenster rau' Tommi sieht gar lustig aus

Page from Peter Einstein's scrapbook showing the flat rented by his parents in Chorlton-cum-Hardy in south Manchester.

DER WEG UND SOMMERAUFEN HALT DER AUSREISER EINSTEI

DIE „AMSTERDAM"

Peter Einstein arrived in Manchester with his parents as a refugee in 1939 at the age of ten and immediately began a scrap book to record his experiences. This page shows the boat and the journey from Chemnitz to Britain. In later life he became a research engineer.

Page from Peter Einstein's scrapbook.

direction and helps more than anything else to make the girls content and happy.

Our dear Granny

The Matron

Page from the 'Harris House Diary' showing the matron at the Harris House refugee hostel in Southport and her mother, both also refugees.

EINE LUFTFAHRT DIE IST LUSTIG " " " " SCHÖN " " " " USW

ACH WIE WARS IN DEUTSCHLAND SCHÖN DOCH ICH MÖCHTS NICHT WIEDER SEHN

Page from the Harris House diary, in which refugees at the hostel recorded their first year in Britain.

Holocaust Survivors

Those who remained in Manchester were joined after 1945 by perhaps 200 survivors of the Nazi genocide, also helped by the Jewish Refugees Committee which, under the energetic chairmanship of Mrs Rae Barash, remained in existence until 1949. Some survivors arrived as individuals through family connections, others as part of a group of 'Boys' allowed into Britain in 1945 and residing at first at a hostel at Windermere in the Lake District. Those who subsequently moved on to Manchester organised themselves into a branch of the Forty-Five Aid Society, both for collective support and to promote, with their Manchester-born children, the 'message' of the Holocaust – 'Never again' – to succeeding generations. They still see themselves, at an older age, as 'the Boys'. As individuals, refugees from Nazism and Holocaust survivors, the largest addition to the Jewish population in the 1930s and 1940s, have now taken their place in the city and the community. Henry Guterman, who arrived in Manchester as a youngster from Berlin shortly before the war, played an important role in linking the Jewish community to Manchester's more recent immigrant groups and in promoting interracial harmony until his death in 2007. He was also the first refugee to become president of the Jewish Representative Council.

Members of the Young Communist League, most of them Jewish, selling the YCL paper The Challenge *in Strangeways, c.1937. They were raising funds to support the International Brigade in Spain.*

Members of the Three Courts Club, a Jewish social club in Manchester, in Blackpool in the 1940s. (Courtesy Manchester Jewish Museum.)

Victory Party on Sunday 19 August 1945 in Maude Street, Hightown. (Courtesy Manchester Jewish Museum.)

Manchester premier of the film 'Mr.Emanuel', based on one of Louis Golding's novels. (Courtesy Manchester Jewish Museum.)

Refugees from the Arab world

Later refugees from the Arab world, particularly from Iran, Iraq, Aden and Egypt, were far fewer in number, therefore their collective impact was less visible. Among the Iranians, however, was David Alliance, who arrived in Britain in 1951 and who, after making his way in the textile trade, became involved in the creation of Coats Viyella, one of the world's largest textile firms. In Manchester his philanthropic activities included the funding of the Nicky Alliance Centre, at first as a social centre for the Jewish Blind Society, and financial support for a Professorship in Modern Jewish Studies at the University of Manchester, as the basis for the establishment of a now flourishing Centre for Jewish Studies. Moroccan refugees established the Nefusot Yehuda Synagogue and the Pinto Yeshiva in north Manchester.

Manchester and Soviet Jewry

One of the unforeseen consequences of Israel's victory in the Six Day War was the stimulus it created for further emigration from the Diaspora to what was seen as the increasingly secure and triumphant Jewish State. Jews of the Soviet Union, long denied dignity in their own country, saw Israel as the land in which

Front page of the Manchester [Jewish] Free Gazette*, 28 January 1949.*

Demonstration in Manchester staged by the Manchester Council for Soviet Jewry.

they might now recover pride in their identity. From the Soviet authorities, still tainted by anti-Semitism, hostile to Israel and fearing the humiliation of an exodus of its citizens, they met with only obstructions and discrimination. The sympathies of the Jewish world, particularly strong in Manchester, went out to these refuseniks.

In 1970 Leslie Donn, then president of the Jewish Representative Council, set up the Manchester Council for Soviet Jewry 'to provide comfort and help for Jews in the USSR during their endured period of refusenikship.' The Council achieved a high degree of efficiency under the chairmanship of Sir Sidney Hamburger, maintaining contact with refuseniks and easing their departure by whatever means were at its disposal. Among the more militant bodies to emerge subsequently in Manchester was a strong local branch of the '35 Society', a body of women who, among other things, organised well-publicised demonstrations outside the local venues of visiting groups from the USSR.

Chapter 13

Manchester Jewry Today

Estimates of the size of the Jewish community at the beginning of the 21st century vary between 25 and 35,000. Such figures, at best guesstimates, may be taken to refer to those who are Jewish in terms of Jewish Law or in their attachment to Jewish institutions. If all those people of Jewish *origin* were to be included, the number would be at least twice as large, for a minority of Jewish settlers in Manchester have been marrying Christians (only some of whom converted to Judaism), or for other reasons abandoning the Jewish faith or distancing themselves from the community, since the late 18th century. It is a tribute to Jewish leaders, lay and religious, and to the strength of religious traditions within a majority of Jewish families, that a religiously observant community has not only survived, but multiplied. Since the early 1970s, in spite of the physical mobility of the Jewish population and its increasing exposure to Britain's secular culture, the level of its religious observance has deepened.

'Stenecourt' in Crumpsall, the successor to the Manchester Great Synagogue, which was finally vacated in 1975. (Courtesy Mike Poloway.)

The Jewish Population

In the post-war years, the movement of the Jewish population to the north and south of the city increased in pace and extent. To the south, commemorated by Hymie Gouldman's nostalgic play, *From Cheetham Hill to Cheadle*, the Jewish population moved southwards in one direction from Didsbury into the Cheshire townships of Cheadle and Gatley and, in another, through Sale and Altrincham and out towards the substantial and mostly Victorian properties of Bowdon and Hale. In the north, while a substantial Jewish population remains in Crumpsall, Prestwich and Higher Broughton, other families moved outwards towards Whitefield and Bury. The movement in both directions, and the circumstances of the Jewish collision with the British petty bourgeoisie, was the subject of sharp satire in the 'Haimisha Pantomimes' of the local writer, Julie Emmanuel performed by the Jewish Amateur Operatic Society, with titles such as *Down at the Old Barmitzvah* and *Cinderelly*.

Synagogues marked the routes and the stages of the Jewish advance. In Cheadle, after worshipping at the local Friends Meeting House, a house at the corner of Altrincham Road and Kingsway was converted in 1964 into the Yeshurun Synagogue which, in 1966, absorbed the by then defunct Stockport congregation. In May 1966 a synagogue (a so-called 'synagogue for the Space Age') was built in Hesketh Road, Sale, for what were then the 120 families living in Sale, Altrincham and Urmston. A synagogue in Hale was opened by the Chief Rabbi in 1981. In 2002 the South Manchester Synagogue in Wilbraham Road, well out of walking distance of its members, was abandoned by its congregants (to be converted into a Jewish Study Centre), who moved to a fine new building in Bowdon. The adjoining suburbs of Bowdon and Hale house one of the fastest growing Jewish communities in Britain. Currently preparations are underway for the construction in Hale of a synagogue for Sephardi families who have made the same southwards journey from Didsbury.

The Yeshurun Synagogue in Cheadle. (Courtesy Manchester Jewish Museum.)

The interior of
Stenecourt Synagogue.
(Courtesy Mike
Poloway.)

In the north, in 1954 the Romanian Synagogue (which in 1942, with Romania an ally of Nazi Germany, had diplomatically changed its name to the North Salford) moved to new premises in Vine Street, Prestwich. In 1956 the North Manchester Synagogue (the former Brodyer Shool) moved from Strangeways into a converted Methodist Church on Leicester Road, where it was joined in later years by the Beth Jacob Synagogue from Hightown and, in 1978, by the Central Synagogue from Heywood Street. The United Synagogue moved from its home in a converted Methodist Chapel, where it had thrived since 1904, to new premises in Meade Hill Road. The Higher Broughton, its

The Bowdon Synagogue
in The Firs, Bowden,
successor to the South
Manchester Synagogue
in Wilbraham Road.
(Courtesy Mike
Poloway.)

Interior of the Bowdon Synagogue. (Courtesy Mike Poloway.)

numbers in steep decline, closed its doors, demolished its building and amalgamated with the Higher Crumpsall in 1969. In 1974 the Great and New Synagogues, now long reunited, moved en bloc to the Great's former 'Crumpsall branch' at Stenecourt. The last surviving synagogue of the old Jewish Quarter, the Spanish and Portuguese, was sold in 1982 to a Jewish Heritage Committee which opened the refurbished building as the Manchester Jewish Museum three years later.

Further north, in 1959 the former old British School on Park Lane was converted into a synagogue for Whitefield's first 80 Jewish families, to be replaced on the same site in 1968 by the Whitefield Hebrew Congregation. In the mid-1960s, plans were set in motion to provide synagogal accommodation for the Jewish families from Cheetham and Hightown, which had settled in and around the Sunnybank estate on the outer edge of Bury. A prefabricated synagogue built in only five days, on the junction of Sunnybank and Manchester Road in September 1965, gave way in 1971 to the new Bury Synagogue, with a seating

The Bury Synagogue. (Courtesy Mike Poloway.)

capacity of 600. In the early 1970s, on the nearby Hillock Estate in Whitefield, around 100 Jewish families, mostly displaced by the demolition of Hightown, began holding services in a private house before moving to the purpose-built Hillock Hebrew Congregation in Ribble Drive.

The Manchester Orthodox

While the level of observance of the middle-of-the-road Orthodox has deepened dramatically since the 1970s, there has been an even more spectacular development in what is often described in popular parlance as ultra-orthodoxy, but which is more properly defined as the stricter (and, in their eyes, more authentic) observance of the *haredim* (the 'God fearers'). Machzikei Hadass ('those who firmly adhere to the Torah'), founded in 1925 by a small group of Eastern European businessmen, has since become the epicentre of an haredi community reinforced after 1956 by Orthodox refugees from Hungary. With their typically large families, and the return of many middle-of-the-road Orthodox families to stricter observance, the haredim are now estimated to constitute 7,000 individuals, making up perhaps a quarter of the religious community. Their historian, Dr Zalkind Yaacov Wise, has argued convincingly that by 2050 the haredim will constitute a communal majority.

While constituting a 'community within a community' (literally an 'austritt gemeinde' or independent community) with its own synagogues, rabbinate, burial boards, Beth Din, Shechita, mikvas, burial ground, shops and agencies of welfare, society and culture, and reviving Yiddish as a distinctive lingua franca, the haredim have also served, by their example, to strengthen the observance of the Orthodox community as a whole. It is also a close-knit society, now expanding beyond its original area of residence in Broughton and Sedgley Park to the King's Road area of Prestwich, based on homes, neighbourhood networks, synagogues and single-sex social and cultural organisations. It has its own 'economy', which meets the particular needs generated by its Orthodox standards, chiefly through shops and services on Leicester Road in Salford or King's Road, Prestwich, which now serve more generally as the heartland of Orthodox retailing and catering. A newsletter, the *Haimischer Advertiser*, publicises haredi businesses, prominent among which are home-based concerns set up and managed by haredi women, whose husbands spend a good deal of

Hale Synagogue, 1981. (Courtesy Mike Poloway.)

time in prayer and religious study, and who are themselves bound to the home by the number of their children. In the strictest Orthodox homes, contact with secular modernity is severely limited. Television ('a sewer running through the house', according to one haredi commentator) is forbidden, there are no secular newspapers and the only novels are those from haredi publishing houses.

'Modernisation'

While religious practice has tended to move in a traditional direction, the institutions of the community generally have become more 'modern'. The movement of the general Jewish population towards the suburbs was as much psychological as physical. It represented, in the first place, the higher social expectations of members of a new Jewish generation. They were effectively turning their backs not only on a Jewish Quarter in a rapid process of physical decline, but on what were, from their new suburban perspective, its antiquated institutions. Charitable, educational and social bodies, once cherished and financially supported, now came to appear too ramshackle in their physical state, too remote, and too outdated in their methods for suburbanising Jewish families. It was not only that these families wanted to take their institutions with them, but they wanted those institutions to be 'modernised'. This was increasingly the case as Jewish communal institutions became eligible for government and civic grants. They now had to prove their efficacy, their professionalism and their capacity to

Halberstadt's butcher's shop, Leicester Road. (Courtesy Mike Poloway.)

manage their institutions efficiently. They had equally to show that the work they were undertaking was not duplicated by other communal institutions. The time when institutions could rely only on amateur managers and volunteers to promote the status or power of their founders was over. Only with the elimination of 'macherism' could the community's 'bureaucratic anarchy' be overcome. Thus, not without resistance from some of those institutions whose personal overlords or cherished independence were under threat, the community 'modernised'.

This became particularly the case as figures emerged within the community who were professionally qualified men and women with experience of working with the civic and national authorities and who were in touch with the latest developments in national welfare and educational work. It was only people of this stamp who were able to identify the inefficiency of communal

The Menorah Synagogue of the North Cheshire Hebrew Congregation, the first Reform Synagogue in south Manchester. (Courtesy Mike Poloway.)

institutions and the 'gaps' left in their provision. One such figure was Ivan Lewis, a qualified social worker, whose career and political ambition took him from the management of Manchester Jewish Social Services (the new title of the Jewish Board of Guardians), to membership of Bury Urban District Council and, finally in 1997, to membership of Parliament, in the Labour interest, for the constituency of Bury North, and into junior ministerial roles in the Labour Government. Another was Howard (now Sir Howard) Bernstein who, after a career in local government, became chief executive of Manchester City Council in 1998.

Ivan Lewis was at first especially concerned to bring order to communal welfare work. Since World War One there had been periodic attempts to coordinate Jewish charity work by bringing together the Jewish Board of Guardians and the Jewish Benevolent Society, whose work had always overlapped, and establishing a 'community chest' which would attract all charitable donations and so replace the separate and often competing fundraising work of particular institutions. The idea of a 'community chest' proved unrealistic. It required a man with the prestige and drive of Ivan Lewis to bring about a rationalisation of communal charity. In April 1997, largely through Lewis's diplomatic efforts, and with the support of his Manchester colleagues, the Board of Guardians and the Benevolent Society were finally amalgamated under a new title, the Manchester Jewish Federation (otherwise the Fed), and their activities 'rationalised'. The Fed's present team of professional workers (not all of them Jewish) and 400 volunteers now provide, with financial assistance from the state, an estimated 3,000 'needy' Jewish people in Manchester with community care, sheltered housing, home help, luncheon clubs, play schemes, a 'toy library', meals on wheels, bereavement support, respite care and a drop-in centre for those recovering from mental illness.

New building at the Brookvale Settlement. (Courtesy Mike Poloway.)

The Nicky Alliance Day Care Centre in Middleton Road, Crumpsall. (Courtesy Mike Poloway.)

The Home for Aged, Sick and Incurables Jews was caught up in the same wave of change initiated, in its case, from within its own Board of Management. First its name was shortened and modernised to 'Jewish Homes for the Aged'. Then, in 1959, when the now ramshackle home on Cheetham Hill Road and its newer branch on Leicester Road were full to overflowing, the decision was taken to purchase a mansion off Moor Lane in Prestwich called Heathlands, set in four and a half acres of land, for the construction of a 'Home for our Senior Citizens worthy of this Generation'. The first turf was cut in July 1965 by Jacob Rothschild, building began in 1969 and, in 1972, Heathlands Village was opened to its first elderly residents. The name itself was chosen to suggest that the new home was 'free of institutional atmosphere', that it offered a range of facilities beyond simple care and medical treatment, and that its intent was to accord to its residents a new level of 'dignity'. Now, in its own words, 'the premier Jewish Care Home in the North of England' and, in public estimation, among the best in Britain, Heathlands Village is run by a trained staff of over 250 and 100 volunteers. Apart from beautifully designed rooms, shops, services and an in-house synagogue, it has on offer 42 flats for 'independent living' and a special care unit 'for residents with Alzheimer's and Dementia'.

Among the most evident gaps in the welfare provision of the Jewish community before 1945 was the lack of facilities for the visually impaired and for the mentally or physically handicapped. The Jewish blind needing residential care had no choice but to find a place in Henshaw's Blind Institute, a Christian body in which they faced food which was *treife*, isolation from their coreligionists and the absence of facilities for Jewish worship and observance. The Jewish mentally handicapped, as much a marginalised group in the community as in the city, were typically placed in homes at some distance from Manchester where they faced similar dangers. Both are now provided for within the community, the blind by a society set up by the businessman Louis Glasky, and now incorporated into Manchester Jewish Community Care, the handicapped by the Brookvale Settlement, another modern institution established in Simister Lane, Prestwich. A third organisation, Outreach, offers residential facilities within the community for those recently discharged from mental hospitals and homes for the mentally handicapped.

Jewish philanthropists, local and national, have identified themselves with the processes of modernisation. The Nicky Alliance Centre, set up with the support of David Alliance as a day care centre for the Jewish visually impaired, has subsequently served the elderly, the lonely and all those 'with visual impairment, physical disability, or suffering from a dementia-related illness'.

Welcome desk at the Nicky Alliance Centre. (Courtesy Mike Poloway.)

Drill session of the Jewish Lads' and Girls' Brigade. (Courtesy Manchester Jewish Museum.)

Jewish Education

Since World War Two, which added a new urgency to the survival of Judaism, Jewish education in Manchester has become at once more 'modern' and more 'traditional'. A key figure has been another Jewish businessman, Joshua Rowe, who in 1990, at the suggestion of the then Chief Rabbi Lord Jacobovits, investigated the role of the King David Junior and High Schools, which in 1959 had replaced the Manchester Jews' School, in safeguarding the Jewish identity in Manchester. He discovered that, whereas the Junior School was functioning effectively, at secondary level, Jewish parents were preferring to send their children to Manchester Grammar School or the Manchester High School for Girls, both with strong academic reputations, rather than to King David's High. The result, he believed, was to compound the religious erosion of the Jewish community already taking place on a substantial scale through intermarriage, assimilation and apathy. What was required was a regeneration of the High School as a centre of both secular and religious learning. As a hands-on chairman of the school's Board of Governors, this is what he attempted to achieve, partly by tightening up policies on discipline, dress code and homework, by creating a sixth-form with dedicated teachers, class tutors and

The North Cheshire Jewish Primary School, a junior school in Cheadle with a 'modern Orthodox' ethos. (Courtesy Mike Poloway.)

mentors, by introducing streaming, and by building up a cadre of 116 highly qualified specialist teachers, in part by setting up an experimental branch of the school which he called Yavneh. In time, by these means, he dispelled the High School's sense of failure and created a revitalised institution increasingly attractive to aspiring Jewish parents. The number of children at the High School increased from around 200 in 1991, when there were real fears of the school's closure, to 870 by 2007.

Yavneh was a particular success, both in its own right and as a pacesetter for the whole King David Campus. Advertised at the time of its foundation in 1997 as 'an exclusive educational unit' providing 'a modern orthodox Jewish education for girls at secondary level', a boys' equivalent was added in 2002. 'Modern orthodox' meant strict observance of Jewish law allied to an engagement with modernity in matters of everyday dress, occupation and social custom and an allegiance to Zionism. So Yavneh, while engendering an appreciation of Orthodox Judaism and delivering a curriculum which combined Ivrit (modern Hebrew), Jewish studies and secular subjects, promotes 'the centrality of Israel' in Jewish society. The intention, now fully achieved, was to set standards of academic excellence which would serve as exemplars for those of the High School as a whole, while the ethos of 'modern orthodoxy' might be expected to filter through to the rest of the campus. It was seen equally as an incentive to the teaching staff to draw out the highest standards of which the students were capable. The King David graduate, Rowe believed, should be equally at home in the world of Jewish learning and in the British centres of academic excellence to which he expected the more able students to aspire. The new King David's would also have a social mission. To encourage students 'to show concern for others', social projects became 'an important and integral aspect of school life', student volunteers being encouraged to work with communal charities. King David's is now in the top tier of British secondary

Class at Yavneh School on the King David Campus. (Courtesy Mike Poloway.)

schools in terms of academic achievement, is delivering students to a wide range of British universities and has begun to produce, as Rowe hoped it would, a new cadre of communal leaders.

Much of this achievement, and a significant proportion of its cost, must be attributed to Joshua Rowe, who remains in daily contact with the school. As chairman (and later president) of the main Zionist fundraising body in Manchester, the United Joint Israel Appeal, he personally canvassed its subscribers (often on a door-to-door basis) on the advantages of the King David High, persuading many to see it as the first choice for the education of the children. His decision to include his own daughter among the first entrants to Yavneh encouraged others to back his judgement.

Joshua Rowe would describe his own religious position, and the religious ethos of King David High, as modern orthodox: the form of strict observance which, unlike that of most haredim, allows for a substantial engagement with cultural modernity, including mixed-gender schools, and which has encouraged an attachment to Zionism. Its equivalent for younger pupils is the North Cheshire Jewish Primary School.

Orthodox rabbi with his students. (Courtesy Mike Poloway.)

The revival of King David Campus as a centre of educational excellence, and the progress of the North Cheshire Primary School, has been paralleled by the equally impressive evolution of single-sex primary and secondary schools in which the teaching and codes of behaviour are suited to the more strictly Orthodox sectors of the community and which have been equally seeded by communal philanthropists, some of them haredi. They include, in particular, the Jewish Grammar School for Boys (first established in 1959, and now the Manchester Mesivta) and the Jewish High School for Girls (now Beth Yaacov), both of which have moved into ultra-modern new buildings, the one in Charlton Avenue, Prestwich, the other on Bury New Road. The secondary school, Bnos Yisrael (founded in 1965 with six girls, and now with 500 pupils) is located on Leicester Road, and the primary schools, Yesoiday Ha Torah (with 566 pupils) and the Broughton Jewish Cassel-Fox School (with 280), first established in 1943 in the premises of the former refugee hostel, are situated on Upper Park Road. Thus there now exists in Manchester a range of primary and secondary schools, all offering high standards of academic education, meeting the needs, pockets (in otherwise free schools, parents pay for the Hebrew education of their children) and religious preferences of every sector of the Orthodox community.

Since the early 1960s, boys and girls leaving Orthodox schools have been encouraged to go on for one or two years to a boys' Yeshiva or a girls' Seminary, either in Gateshead, the United States or Israel, before going on to university and settling to a career or marriage.

Outside communal schools, Darryl Lee, a member of Manchester Maccabi (in origin a Zionist sports organisation), raised funds for the construction of the Manchester Maccabi Community and Sports Club (now the Brooklands Centre), which opened in September 2006 as a recreational and social centre for Jewish youth. Currently made up of meeting rooms, a restaurant and a recreational hall, the intention is to raise further funds to create tennis courts, football pitches and facilities for a full range of indoor and outdoor sports.

In general terms, the community's 'inner structure' of education and welfare remains in place but, while it continues to demand the support of volunteers, subscriptions and donations from within the community, and is designed to take account of the religious susceptibilities of Jewish people, it now increasingly works in partnership with government agencies, from which it receives a degree of financial aid. It is now perhaps best described as the 'Jewish sector' of the welfare state.

'Community First'

Within the community there has also been a decisive move recently towards the long-term planning of the community's needs. This was again initiated by Ivan Lewis who, in the late 1990s, wrote a paper stressing the need for strategic thinking and suggesting a communal 'commission' to achieve it. After some discussion (and not a little scepticism) and with the support of Sir Howard Bernstein and David Arnold, then president of the Jewish Representative Council, a commission of 10 members was put together (now known as the Bernstein Commission) to consider the community's needs and how they might be met. After preliminary research conducted by the Business School of Aston University, which included interviews with major figures in Jewish communal life, a Community First organisation (based on the notion that each communal organisation should think first about the needs of the community as a whole) was brought into being under the chairmanship of Sir Howard Bernstein and with representatives of every sector of the

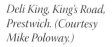

Deli King, King's Road, Prestwich. (Courtesy Mike Poloway.)

Hyman's Delicatessen,
Leicester Road.
(Courtesy Mike
Poloway.)

community, including four haredi rabbis. Although the setting up of Community First was clearly a declaration of intent by communal leaders, it is too early to speculate on what it might achieve in terms of the modernisation and rationalisation of the community's institutions. It held its first meeting in May 2007.

Equally linked to the future development of Manchester Jewry has been the setting up by the Representative Council in May 2007 of 'New Leadership', a series of annual courses intended 'to breathe new life into the leadership of the community'.

The Religious Complexion of the Community

Outside the Jewish Orthodox, whether haredi or 'modern', are members of the Reform Synagogue, which still flourishes, and 'secular Jews', whose Jewish identity might be expressed solely, for example, by membership of the Jewish Socialist Group, the Jewish Gay and Lesbian Alliance or one or other of Manchester's Zionist formations, or simply by a sense of sharing with people of common origin. When the original Reform Synagogue, designed by Edward Salomon, was destroyed in the Blitz of 1941, its congregation worshipped at first in a prefab specially built on the Park Place site, then in a public hall near the city centre, until a new synagogue was opened in Jackson's Row, off Albert

Sign for the Muslim-Jewish Forum at Manchester Town Hall. (Courtesy Mike Poloway.)

Square, in November 1954. A year later it had attracted a membership of 700. During the 1950s, new concentrations of Reform families emerged in Cheadle and in Whitefield. For the Cheadle Reformers, the Menorah Synagogue in Sharston was built for the North Cheshire Reform Congregation and opened in 1972. For the Whitefield Reform families, temporary synagogal accommodation in Elm Street, acquired in 1976, was later converted into a new synagogue, the Sha'arei Shalom. Within the last few years, Liberal Judaism has made its first appearance in Manchester in the shape of a group of families, yet more distant from traditional orthodoxy than the Reformers, who are currently meeting for Sabbath service in the Friends Meeting House or the Cross Street Unitarian Chapel in central Manchester.

As the Manchester haredim have gained in size, confidence and assertiveness, especially in the face of the British social and cultural revolution of the late 1960s, their relationship with Reform Judaism, never close, has soured. Much the same is true of the less strict orthodox congregations now aspiring to greater observance. Reform rabbis are not recognised as such by their orthodox peers. Conversions to Judaism effected by the Reform Movement are not seen as valid. Tense relations and occasional conflict between the Reformers and the Othodox mark the extreme of what has become, in religious terms, a polarised community. The haredim themselves, however, are united only in terms of the strictness of their observance, their suspicion of 'modernity' and their opposition to secular Zionism. Within haredi Manchester, there are currently members of eight different hassidic sects, each with its own stiebl and study centre, each giving allegiance to a different dynasty of rebbes, usually with their headquarters in the United States, as well as strictly Orthodox *misnagdim*, with their own synagogues and a Yeshiva, based on Lithuanian traditions, the Shaarei Torah on Upper Park Road in Broughton Park. Most haredim are concerned chiefly with their own conduct, although some see themselves as exemplars of authentic orthodoxy. Of all the chassidim, it is only the Lubavitchers who have an outreach programme which seeks, through its emissaries, to raise the general standards of observance within the Manchester community. At the same time, haredi rabbis of differing hassidic allegiance (as the source of rabbinical guidance in Eastern Europe was destroyed in the Holocaust) compose the ministry of most Orthodox synagogues in Manchester and it is through their functions as congregational officials that they are able to move their congregants in the direction of greater observance.

Hanuciah at the junction of Cheetham Hill Road and Leicester Road, placed by the Lubavitcher Chassids. (Courtesy Mike Poloway.)

Sign on a Manchester street, placed by the Lubavitcher Chassids. (Courtesy Mike Poloway.)

The Jews and Others

The Jewish community has, from its beginnings, inevitably been concerned about its relationship with those outside its boundaries, and particularly with a majority community within which anti-Semitism persists. One of the major objectives of the Jewish Representative Council has been (and remains) the protection of the community from anti-Semitic assault, most frequently by negotiation with the local authorities. Since the escalation of anti-Zionism, some of it with anti-Semitic overtones, and of such anti-Semitic incidents as the desecration of Jewish burial grounds, the harassment of Jewish people and the vandalising of Jewish buildings, the community, locally and nationally, has necessarily become more concerned for the physical well-being of its members. One symptom of this anxiety has been the setting up in Manchester, in 2004, of a Northern regional branch of the nationwide Community Security Trust. The Trust publicises anti-Semitic incidents, advises Jewish institutions on their own defence, liaises with the police and provides guards at the venues of Jewish events likely to attract hostility.

The community has also become aware of itself as one of several ethnic groups in Manchester which have experienced hostility on the grounds of race or religion. A central figure in emphasising this shared experience and in promoting inter-ethnic harmony was the late Henry Guterman, a refugee to Manchester from Nazi Germany, who had learnt from his experience of Nazi persecution of the tragedy of racism, and who was president of the Manchester Jewish Representative Council from 1986 to 1989. It was Guterman who initiated the first Jewish-Black Forum in Manchester and who went on to set up an Indian-Jewish Association, of which he was joint chairman. His influence, and his friendship with the Manchester City Councillor and one time Lord Mayor Afzal Khan, was also an important factor in the establishment of a Muslim-Jewish Forum. Another organisation which promotes Jewish-Muslim dialogue is Salaam-Shalom, at present an informal committee working in the Prestwich-Bury area which is home to both. Following Guterman's death in June 2007, his ideals have been taken on board by the

'Happy Chanukah' sign on Manchester Town Hall. (Courtesy Mike Poloway.)

Jewish Representative Council, which is linked to inter faith groups and to the Council of Christians and Jews, of which Guterman was vice-chairman. What remains the largest and most vibrant of provincial Jewish communities is now also engaged in making Britain a safer home for all minorities. The Manchester Jewish Museum, which began as a celebration of the Manchester Jewish Heritage, is presently in the course of creating a complementary Centre of Tolerance on its Cheetham site.

Chapter 14

History and Heritage

In the face of changing social, economic and cultural forces, towns and cities throughout Britain are in a constant state of change. Manchester, in particular, is currently undergoing a process of radical regeneration, led and controlled by the planners of the City Council, but including extensive private enterprise. For city dwellers, there is much to admire in the new cultural amenities and living spaces which are evolving. For the historian, it is also a time of anxiety, as the new shapes created on the ground by the bulldozers of redevelopment threaten the physical heritage of the city. Some of it is destroyed, some of it transformed. So the Manchester Free Trade Hall, once the temple of Manchester's Free Traders, and the venue of meetings which have changed the course of the city's history, while retaining its original external shape, has been reinvented as a five-star hotel. Whole districts are being demolished to make way for blocks of luxury flats or new industrial plants.

The former site of the first Jewish settlement in Manchester in the 1780s. The new Urbis Centre is in the foreground; behind it, what remains of long Millgate. (Courtesy Mr Merton Paul.)

Red Bank in the course of redevelopment. The area is to be covered by blocks of flats, a hotel and other facilities. (Courtesy Mr Merton Paul.)

What is happening today is, of course, no more than a speeding up of the general processes of urban change. Historical sites in Manchester have been giving way to the progressive and inexorable 'modernisation' of housing, industry, leisure and retail trading since the end of the 18th century. So the first Manchester Jewish community of the 1780s took shape in what had once been the prosperous centre of an emerging town, but which was then giving way in the face of new industries and an expanding population. What in the mid-19th century became the Jewish Quarter, in Strangeways and Cheetham Hill, was built around the decaying mansions of what had once been a desirable and semi-rural suburb. In the late 19th century Jewish immigrants from Eastern Europe 'invaded' English inner suburbs already in the process of decline, converting 'native' institutions to their own use: the shops, houses and places of worship of a retreating Christian population became the synagogues, clubs, Friendly Societies, workshops, kosher restaurants, gambling dens and Trade Union branches of the newcomers. What, in the 1850s, had been built as the grand and highly ornamented Town Hall of what was then the independent township of Cheetham had, by the 1890s, as Cheetham was absorbed administratively into the city of Manchester, with the nearby Cheetham Assembly Rooms, became the focus of Jewish social, cultural and political life: the venue of Jewish weddings, receptions, fundraising concerts and Zionist bazaars.

*Red Bank cleared and
ready for
redevelopment.
(Courtesy Mr Merton
Paul.)*

*Closing service at the
Great Synagogue, 1974.
(Courtesy Manchester
Jewish Museum.)*

Immigrants are typically both the beneficiaries of change and its victims. Urban change first creates spaces cheap and accessible enough for their settlement, only to finally overwhelm the new societies they have created within and around them. From the years immediately after World War One, the old Jewish Quarter on Cheetham Hill was slowly, at first almost imperceptibly, collapsing.

With the movement of Jewish population 'up the hill' towards Crumpsall and Prestwich, the collapse of the Jewish Quarter was hastened by slum clearance, beginning with Red Bank during 1938–39, the decline of what had been the major immigrant industries (clothing and furniture) after World War Two, and by the subsequent entry into the area of a new generation of immigrants, some Afro-Caribbean, most Pakistanis, Bangladeshis and Indians. So Cheetham Town Hall has begun its third life as an Indian restaurant, Jewish shops, factories and warehouses have come to house Asian manufacturers and traders, and at least one synagogue (the old Central in Heywood Street) has been converted into a mosque. The New Synagogue has been gutted to become an Asian trade warehouse. These 'new immigrants' will, in turn, become subject to the changes brought about by their economic success and higher social expectations and by the processes of urban regeneration, their 'new society' itself giving way and their heritage placed at risk.

The heritage of societies of immigrant origin is thus particularly vulnerable, rendered all the more so in the case of Jewish societies by the religious imperative of families having synagogues within walking distance of

The Great Synagogue shortly before the departure of its congregation and the subsequent vandalisation. (Courtesy Manchester Jewish Museum.)

Hebrew Clock rescued from the defunct Colwyn Bay Hebrew Congregation. (Courtesy Manchester Jewish Museum.)

their homes. As Jewish people move, so do their workplaces and institutions, leaving behind the vulnerable hulks of abandoned synagogues, deserted (and finally demolished) houses and defunct factories. As often as not, artefacts, documents and photographs are dumped or lost. When the Higher Broughton Synagogue was demolished in the mid-1960s, its records were buried in the rubble. Ark curtains once belonging to the synagogue were later retrieved from a flea market more typically devoted to old clothes and household goods and third-rate bric-a-brac. When, in 1974, the congregation of the Manchester Great Synagogue decided to move to a more convenient site in Crumpsall, the precautions taken by its officials were insufficient to prevent the extensive vandalisation of the building and the theft or destruction of such artefacts as the pulpit, the pews, the candelabra which once stood before the Ark and the copper domes which once graced the exterior of a listed building. When, in 1967, a room in what were then the headquarters of the local Zionist movement was used for the storage of jewellery donated to the cause of Israel, the papers which 'cluttered' the room were deposited on the local tip. Thus, in one blow, the records of Zionist organisations which had been active in Manchester since the 1880s were lost, as if one new layer of communal history were eliminating the layers below it. And when the evidence of history disappears, so do the

Teapot made by Lipton's. (Courtesy Manchester Jewish Museum.)

Philanthropic Hall, which once housed the Jewish Soup Kitchen, boarded up ready for redevelopment, probably as an Asian radio station. (Courtesy Mr Merton Paul.)

experiences and achievements of those who made that history, so that, for example, the complete history of Manchester Zionism can only be reconstructed from references in the press and the autobiographical fragments of its pioneers.

The opening of the Manchester Jewish Museum, in a Moorish building on Cheetham Hill Road which had once been the Spanish and Portuguese Synagogue, had the immediate objective of creating a focus for the rescue of what remained of the Jewish heritage. With the help of English Heritage, Manchester City and Greater Manchester Councils and a host of private donors, the building was purchased, restored and converted into a museum which first opened in 1984. The original layout of the synagogue was retained and enhanced, with only the Ladies Gallery of what had been an Orthodox place of worship being converted into a display area

The National School of Chiropody and Free Foot Hospital on Bury New Road, c.1930. The building was originally the Beth Hamedrash attached to the North Manchester Synagogue. Part of the same building is now a section of the Pakistani firm 'Joe Bloggs Jeans'. (Courtesy Manchester Jewish Museum.)

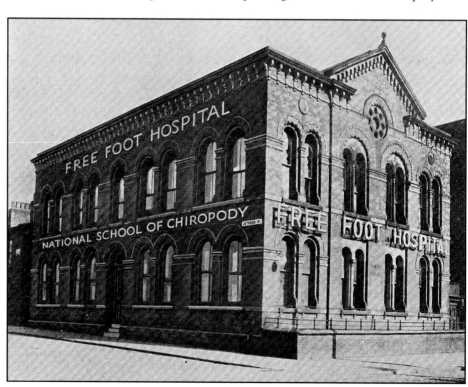

The Ladies Gallery of the Spanish and Portuguese Synagogue in the course of repair and conversion into the permanent exhibition of the Manchester Jewish Museum. (Courtesy Manchester Jewish Museum.)

Group in the Succah of the Spanish and Portuguese Synagogue shortly before its conversion into the exhibition gallery of the Manchester Jewish Museum. (Courtesy Manchester Jewish Museum.)

Exhibit in the Manchester Jewish Museum, 'The immigrant trades,' showing a bench used by a waterproof garment maker. (Courtesy Manchester Jewish Museum.)

TOP RIGHT: Interior of the Manchester Jewish Museum, the former Spanish and Portuguese Synagogue. (Courtesy Manchester Jewish Museum.)

which now houses a history of Manchester Jewry. This is made up of photographs, reconstructions, artefacts, documents and extracts from interviews with Jewish people, all of which the museum has retrieved. Its collecting policy extended far beyond the ceremonial silver of Jewish synagogues. The museum sought to rescue and display items of any kind which lent substance to the everyday experiences in the home, the workplace or the neighbourhood, of Jewish Mancunians of the past. Currently it holds a collection of over 500 tape recordings of Jewish people and 10,000 photographs, many copied from the personal albums of Jewish families, some reproduced in this book. What had once been the *Succah*, a small hall at the rear of the synagogue formerly reserved for the celebration of the Festival of Tabernacles, is now a gallery housing temporary exhibitions on Jewish themes. In the museum's storeroom are some of the many items recovered by a process of rescue to which the museum remains committed.

While the museum has developed a strong educational programme which extends to schools and adult groups, Jewish and non-Jewish, within the region and beyond, and a wide-ranging calendar of cultural events, it remains, in alliance with the museums and libraries of the city, the custodian and the protector of the Manchester Jewish heritage which this book has attempted to illustrate.

Glossary

Alrightnik
Nickname given in the Yiddish press to Jews of Eastern European origin who made rapid economic progress in British society.

Ashkenazi (-im)
Jews originating in Central, Western and Eastern Europe, whose common vernacular language was Yiddish.

Barmitzvah
Ritual for boys coming of age at 13. In some synagogues, a similar ritual has been devised for girls.

Beth Din
Rabbinical court for the interpretation of Jewish Law.

Beth Hamedrash
House of Study, often attached to a synagogue as a place for the study of sacred texts.

Bimah
Platform in a synagogue from which the portion of the law is read during a Jewish service.

Board of Deputies
Properly, the Board of Deputies of British Jews. The national body of representatives set up in London in the 18th century to offer a degree of cohesion to the life and policies of British Jewry and to serve as the Jewish community's mechanism of negotiation with the outside society. Manchester, like other provincial communities, has 'deputies' representing local Jewish institutions.

Chassidism
A movement originating in Eastern Europe in the 18th century, laying greater emphasis on the emotional expression of Judaism. A number of chassidic sects were founded (and mostly still exist), each with its own dynasty of rabbis. Now used more generally, and wrongly, to describe those judged to be haredi or 'ultra' Orthodox. In reality the haredim in Manchester and elsewhere, although a majority are chassidic, include the non-chassidic *misnagdim*.

Cheder (-arim)
Literally, 'room'. Private class for the study of religion and Hebrew.

Chevra (-oth)
Small society set up by Jewish immigrants, usually in a private house, to serve as a place of worship, a social centre and a place from which newcomers might expect advice and financial help. Its affairs would typically be conducted in Yiddish.

Hachsharah (-oth)
Training centre for young Zionists.

Haredi (-im)
Othodox Jew who rejects the compromises made to Jewish codes of behaviour in the interests of acculturation and modernity.

Kosher
Food prepared in accordance with the Jewish dietary laws.

Minyan *(-im)*
Ten male adults required for the celebration of public worship.

Oral Law
Otherwise the *Talmud*. Classical Rabbinical commentaries on the Torah.

Orthodox
Those who follow the more traditional forms of Jewish observance and ritual.

Reader Otherwise **Cantor** or **Chazan**.
The person who, during a Jewish service, reads the portion of the Torah relevant to a particular date.

Reform Movement
The movement for the 'modernisation' of Jewish ritual and the revision of Jewish theology, beginning in Germany in the early 19th century.

Schule or Shool
Common name for a synagogue.

Sephardi (-im)
Jews living in Spain and Portugal in the Middle Ages and who, in the late 15th century, were dispersed throughout the Mediterranean region. Their common language was Ladino.

Shechita
Traditional ritual for the slaughter of cattle and poultry to provide kosher meat.

Shechita Board
Mechanism for controlling the quality and supply of communal kosher meat.

Shochet (-im)
Person properly qualified to slaughter animals according to Jewish law.

Succah
Portion of a synagogue (or separate structure) used for the celebration of the Festival of Tabernacles.

Talmud Torah
Religious school in which children are taught religion and Hebrew up to the age of 13.

Torah
The Holy Law: that is the first five books of the Old Testament. A *Sefer Torah* is the scroll of the Law used in the synagogue service.

Treife
Food judged to be impure under the Jewish dietary laws.

Yeshiva
Academy for higher Jewish learning and rabbinical training.

Zedaka
Traditional obligation on members of a Jewish community to offer help to the communal poor and needy.

Further Reading

Collins, Lydia

The Sephardim of Manchester, Pedigrees and Pioneers Shaare Hayim, The Sephardi Congregation of South Manchester, 2006.

Cesarani, David

The Making of Modern Anglo-Jewry Oxford, 1990.

Endelman, Todd

The Jews of Modern Britain 1656–2000 Los Angeles, 2002.

Gartner, Lloyd

The Jewish Immigrant in England, 1870–1914 London, 1960.

Kadish, Sharman

Jewish Heritage in England: an architectural guide English Heritage, 2007.

Kushner, Tony

The Jewish Heritage in British History: Englishness and Jewishness London, 1992.

Williams, Bill

The Making of Manchester Jewry, 1740–1875 Manchester University Press, 1976.

Williams, Bill

Sir Sidney Hamburger and Manchester Jewry: Religion, City and Community Frank Cass, 1999.

Index